ALMOST FAMOUS

Recollections

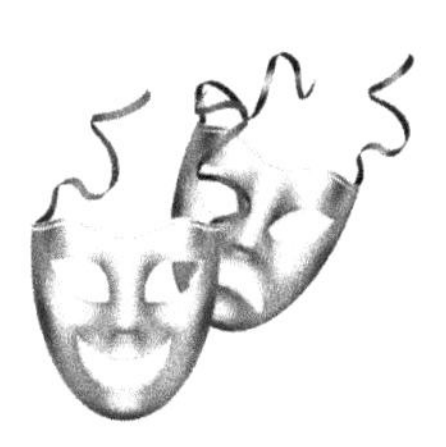

Robin Hawdon

Almost Famous – Recollections
Robin Hawdon

www.robinhawdon.com

This book is sold with the understanding that the author is not offering specific personal or professional advice to the reader. All opinions expressed are solely those of the author, and not offered as conclusive facts. No offence is intended to any person, living or dead. The author disclaims any responsibility for liability, loss or risk, personal or otherwise, that happens as a consequence of the use and application of any of the contents of this book.

Design, cover and publishing support by
www.AuthorSupportServices.com

ISBN: 978-1-922375-06-3 (pbk) 978-1-922375-07-0 (e-book)

A catalogue record for this
book is available from the
National Library of Australia

For all my adventurous and talented family

ALMOST FAMOUS

"Every child is an artist.
The problem is staying an artist when you grow up."
—Pablo Picasso

Contents

PROLOGUE

Let me begin with my favourite poem:-

I will arise and go now, and go to Innisfree,
And a small cabin build there, of clay and wattles made;
Nine bean-rows will I have there, a hive for the honey-bee,
And live alone in the bee-loud glade.

And I shall have some peace there, for peace comes dropping slow,
Dropping from the veils of the morning to where the cricket sings;
There midnight's all a glimmer, and noon a purple glow,
And evening full of the linnet's wings.

I will arise and go now, for always night and day
I hear lake water lapping with low sounds by the shore;
While I stand on the roadway, or on the pavements grey,
I hear it in the deep heart's core.

In most of us there is an impulse that echoes Yeats's yearning for a hermit's retreat to an arcadian existence far from the strains of a fraught world. It is a sentiment that – addicted as I am to the writer's solitary life – often intrudes whenever I see an evocative landscape or isolated cottage, perhaps overlooking the sea. Of course it's a fantasy. How would one handle the laundry in a bee-loud glade, or get access to one's favourite tipple when supplies ran out on Innisfree? Quite apart from being bored to tears within a week.

However the poetic instinct is always there. As Sartre said – 'Hell is other people.'

But then life is other people too.

This is not a genuine autobiography, nor a linear memoir, nor a philosophical treatise. But perhaps a bit of all three. It is a haphazard collection of writings on the various subjects and events that have occupied and inspired me during a fairly turbulent, but hugely fulfilling life. It is a scattering of chapters about the well-known people, the places, the obsessions, and the many different occupations that have filled the more than sixty years I have spent bouncing around the arts, and which have made me almost successful, almost affluent, and almost famous.

The secret of happiness depends on four things. One's biological makeup, which one has from birth, and about which one can do little. One's encounters with the accidents of fate, again which one can rarely avoid. One's own ability and tenaciousness to overcome the trials that life tosses in the way. And finally – and I believe most important of all – one's ability to be *creative*.

Creativity isn't confined to the arts. Creativity applies to everything one does. To one's job, however mundane. To one's habitat, however humble. To one's pastimes, however simple. To one's relationships, however problematic. Creativity is what progresses the universe, and if one isn't contributing to that, then inevitably subconscious dissatisfaction is the result.

It is my own creative urge that has always preserved my optimistic attitude towards my own and humanity's future, in the face of an unrelenting stream of dispiriting news from all corners of the planet, and the bombardment of pessimism from much of the media, and indeed from many of my fellow artists.

I am an octogenarian, an atheist, a hedonist, an introvert, an optimist, and a Conservative (for most of the time). I'm impatient with people, I have a bad memory, I have an IQ of 155 (according to Mensa, which simply means I'm good at certain types of calculation and deduction, and has little to do with actual intelligence), and I almost became James Bond, but thankfully didn't.

According to my wife and daughters I walk too fast, I speak too fast, I drive too fast, I do most things too fast.

I'm intrigued by politics, philosophy, psychology, history, science, and the ways of evolution.

I get immense pleasure – dare I say joy – from my work, my homes, countrysides everywhere, the cinema (more than the stage), great acting, pretty women, funny people from Groucho Marx to Tommy Cooper, Matt cartoons, good restaurants, champagne, golf, fast cars, warm climates, swimming pools, trees, mountains, and beauty in all its forms. I love my wife, my daughters, and my grandchildren, who are all far better human beings than I am (hence my optimism for the future). And, despite all, I both love and despair of myself.

I have been at various times a waiter (failed), a farm hand (failed), a rally driver (failed), a would-be opera singer (failed), a property developer (fairly successful), an actor (fairly successful), a minor film star, a stage director, a theatre director, and a writer.

Mostly a writer. Always a writer since the age of eighteen. A writer of comedies, farces, serious dramas, film scripts, TV scripts, poems, articles, and novels. The fascination with the writing process is something that never leaves me. Writing is perhaps the most creative of all the arts, in that it combines intellect, emotion and aesthetics all at once. Man's writings are the essence of his spirit exposed. Written words, in all their forms, tell the true story of humanity.

I have worked with a lot of genuinely famous people, known a lot of extraordinary characters, done a lot of peculiar things, and some embarrassing ones.

All of which I will touch on in this book. If it never sees the light of publicity, then at least it might enlighten my own descendants a little, and even myself. At any rate it will keep me occupied until an idea for the next proper literary subject arrives.

CHAPTER ONE

Learning

I left my hated boarding school, having taken my scholarship 'A Levels', as they were then known, at the age of eighteen. I had been offered a place at St John's College, Cambridge, but chose instead to go to the Royal Academy Of Dramatic Art, or 'Rada' as the whole world called it. After enduring five years of torment at the all male Uppingham school – caused mostly by my own inability to cope with the rigid disciplines, the monastic existence, and the arcane camaraderie rituals of teenage boys, which I never quite understood – I was desperately keen to experience the bright lights of London, contact with the opposite sex, and an occupation that entailed more stirring activity than academic study.

I had thought up until I was sixteen that I wanted to be a farmer. Fantasies of rounding the sheep across sun-bathed hills, and riding hay wagons over golden fields. But harvest-time blisters and winter muck-spreading soon put an end to that. And farmer's daughters are often hefty-thighed Amazons with laughs like cock-crows (except for the one I eventually married).

It was 1957, and the very first glimpses of the 'swinging sixties' dawn were sparking in the vast capital, still arguably the largest city in the world, and populated by some three hundred ethnic varieties.

Post war rationing was over, female contraception was surfacing, skirts were rapidly shrinking, and 'kitchen sink' drama, written and performed by 'angry young men' was revolutionising the theatre world.

In those days one could park a car almost anywhere on the London streets free of charge, there was no such thing as vehicle MOT certificates, and one could do sixty miles an hour along the Thames Embankment with a bottle of wine inside one, and very little chance of being caught by the cops. Not that I could take advantage of any of those things at that point, impoverished student that I was.

When I announced to my parents that I needed to live in London, rather than commute from our Surrey home thirty miles south, they gave me an allowance of three pounds ten shillings a week. Astonishingly, I was then able, not only to rent a small room in a hilariously eccentric Bed & Breakfast establishment in Islington – run by two old crones who could have been cast as the witches in Macbeth – but also to get to the cinema and the theatre quite frequently, and even dine out once a week or so in the cheap eateries that students are so skilful at discovering. Such are the ways of inflation.

However, I'm getting ahead of myself.

The Royal Academy is a conglomeration of buildings set between Gower Street and Malet Street in the Bloomsbury area of London. The college had progressed under its principal, John Fernald, from being during the previous decades little more than a glorified finishing school for young debutantes, to probably the world's most distinguished theatre school. I had taken the entrance audition there during my last term at school, but so nervous was I on that occasion that I failed to observe much of the surroundings. Now however, having been accepted, I arrived – again nervous, but also expectant – and assessed the situation.

I had anticipated a stately urban palace smelling of history and grease paint, walled with portraits of famous thespians, and thronged with charismatic future stars and stunningly beautiful girls. Instead I found a rather bleak collection of bare classrooms redolent of school, a large canteen (ditto), a couple of musty smelling theatre spaces, and a motley collection of nondescript students, mostly as impecunious as myself, and mostly lacking – on first acquaintance at any rate – in any sort of charisma or beauty.

However I soon learned that true charisma is an internal thing, and that female beauty is something that often reveals itself with familiarity.

Actors are on the whole intelligent, animated, entertaining, and warm-hearted animals. They are also egocentric, emotional, vulnerable and insecure. How else could they be, in what is essentially such a crazy and not very healthy occupation? (more of that later.)

It's a strange thing about actors and actresses (I refuse to call the latter actors. If you called a waitress a waiter, she'd pour the dinner over you). It is never obvious who is going to shine once they get on stage, or show up on the screen. One can rarely tell from their everyday social persona what unique, magnetic, or evocative image they will project when adopting a role. The people of my generation or thereabouts at RADA who went on to become household names, included such greatly diverse personalities as Albert Finney,

Peter O'Toole, Anthony Hopkins, John Hurt, Tom Courtenay, Alan Bates, Richard Briers, Edward Fox, John Thaw, Ian McShane, Sian Phillips, Diana Rigg, Susannah York, Sarah Miles – and more. These became stars and earned a lot of money during their careers. A host of others established themselves as well-known faces, with more-or-less steady careers. The great majority however, left the academy to persevere manfully for a few years, struggling to make a living in a vastly overcrowded profession, and then faded away into more mundane but far more dependable occupations, never to be heard of again.

During their two years there, students studied various esoteric activities, few of which I suspect were of much genuine use in the profession. They learned how to stick on false beards, and apply make-up techniques to heighten cheekbones and widen eyes. They took dancing lessons in baggy tights, in case they ever had to portray Fred Astaire or Nureyev. They took fencing lessons in case they ever had to play Hamlet (which in my case did actually happen a decade later). And they learned voice exercises, which were supposed to improve elocution, and project speech to the back of the Albert Hall.

These latter classes were conducted by a well-known vocal teacher named Clifford Turner, whose deeply resonant voice everyone tried to imitate whilst declaiming various mellifluous ditties:-

"Oh the moon never beams without bringing me dreams
Of the beautiful Annabel Lee.
And the stars never rise but I see the bright eyes
Of the beautiful Annabel Lee..."

and:

"We are the music makers, and we are the dreamers of dreams,
Wandering by lone sea breakers, and sitting by desolate streams..."

In retrospect I believe that the main benefit of attending the college was that we all gradually became steeped in the ways, the plays, the traditions and the folklores, of English speaking theatre through the ages. We acted theatre, we talked theatre, we breathed theatre. We somehow managed, by begging, borrowing, or stealing, to get to see most of the productions playing in London's forty odd mainstream theatres, and dozens of fringe venues. We debated constantly about stage techniques, we impersonated well-known leading actors, we recounted countless myths and stories of untoward happenings in past productions, we rehearsed speeches endlessly in each other's bedsits.

We gradually, and mainly subconsciously, became actors ourselves. Some more than others.

The business of acting is a mysterious process. Unless you are a natural from birth, it is a technique that has to be learnt, just as playing the violin, or painting a portrait has to be learnt. I am often amused when, on my rare visits to see an embarrassingly inept amateur production of one of my plays, I am surrounded afterwards by a bright-eyed cast, thrilled to have the author actually amongst them, all buzzing with enthusiasm about the work they've put into it, and convinced that they were as good as any professional West End cast in the roles. I have to smile and smile, and congratulate them all on the immense effort they've achieved, and escape as soon as possible with their grateful farewells ringing in my ears.

Acting is not really about acting. It's about *reacting*. Reacting genuinely to what the other person has said to you, or to what event has just occurred, or to what the circumstance dictates. It is not about simply pretending to be someone else, but about how *you* would behave if you were to find yourself in that character's shoes. Hence the phrase 'inhabiting the role'. It is about using yourself.

The great actors invariably project the same personality whatever role they are playing. They simply bring their personal responses and emotions to illustrate that character's circumstance. John Gielgud, Paul Scofield, Anthony Hopkins, Judi Dench, Maggie Smith, Julie Walters, and most top film stars, are still in essence themselves, whatever other personage they are supposed to be inhabiting. It's why one often hears members of the public say, "Oh, but so-and-so is always him/her self." Well, yes – that is their strength. That is what people pay to come and see.

Even Laurence Olivier, often described as the greatest actor of his era, was unmistakably Laurence Olivier, however much he experimented with makeup, gesture, and eccentric mannerisms. When he blacked up to play Othello (could that ever happen now?) one still could not mistake that staccato delivery, that distinctive vocal tone, that innate energised ego.

There are rare exceptions. Alec Guinness was in real life a rather bland personality. He was therefore able to paint quite different characters onto that blank canvas. And there are many examples of actors adopting such clever disguises that they are unrecognisable. Yet underneath all the prosthetics and false hair, it is still the performer's subjective reactions which illuminate the part.

Consequently it is essentially a matter of confidence in one's own personality – the ability to utilise one's personal instincts and attributes – that makes the good actor.

I did not especially distinguish myself at RADA. For a long time I did not have that confidence in myself. Partly as a result of a lonely wartime childhood, and partly due to those insecure years at boarding school, I could not bring myself to be totally assured of my own presence on stage. I was often good at auditions and read-throughs – when one has to rely on pure instinct to get through – but then, when it came to actually learning and analysing the part, I would subconsciously chicken out and adopt false attitudes and counterfeit reactions. The times when I knew I *did* perform well were when the part was closest to myself, and I could identify easily with it. Strangely, one of the roles I did feel at home in was that most challenging of all – Hamlet. But perhaps that was because he too was a lost soul, unsure of his own destiny.

I did not leave RADA with any medals of distinction, but I did leave with both an agent and an immediate part in a West End play!

One of the most popular and inspiring teachers at the college was an actor called Peter Barkworth. He taught what was called 'acting technique', and all the students responded eagerly to his weekly classes, and worked hard to excel in them. Peter was then a charming actor in his early thirties, already quite well established in the profession, and performing at night in a long-running West End comedy. He brought a huge enthusiasm and an analytical mind to the job of performing, and would put his students through all kinds of challenging improvisational or interpretive exercises. He even wrote books on the subject.

For some reason – perhaps because of the instinctive ability at improvising which I mentioned – I was one of his favourite pupils. When I was in my final term, and worrying, as was everyone, about finding an agent to represent me, hopefully followed by actual employment out in the real world, Peter came to me and said, "My understudy in the play I'm in is leaving, and they need to replace him. Both to cover me, and play a small role. Would you like me to suggest you?"

I was taken by surprise, and of course said yes. I went in front of the producers to audition, and was hired on the spot. It was probably the easiest employment I ever achieved.

CHAPTER TWO

Acting

Roar Like A Dove by Leslie Storm was a delightful light comedy which had already been playing for over three years at the Phoenix Theatre in Charing Cross Road (a theatre I was to become quite familiar with over the years). In the cast were a number of well known, but not quite mega, stars – Patrick Barr, Faith Brook, David Hutchinson, and Renée Houston. And of course Peter Barkworth.

Peter had a supporting, but very showy part in the play, with one particular scene in which he had centre stage and brought the house down night after night, bemoaning the amount of animal and human procreation going on around him. Part of my job, apart from understudying him and playing a small role in the first act, was to 'run the corner' for the second act. This meant sitting just off stage with the prompt script (never needed after such a long run), and switching cue lights on and off for the various lighting changes and curtain commands. Each night, even after more than three years in the role, Peter would come off after his big scene, and confer in whispers with me as to how it had gone.

He would say such things as, "I didn't get such a big laugh tonight on the first speech – do you think I paused too long before the tag line?" Or, "Should I try doing a double take on seeing

Renée – what do you think?" Such was his enthusiasm for the art of performing, after a spell in a role that would have driven most actors crazy with ennui at the repetition.

I did get to perform the part once, when he was laid low with flu. I had short notice, only being told when I arrived at the theatre, half an hour before curtain up. I was filled with both apprehension and expectancy at being given my chance. Fortunately I knew the part backwards, having listened to Peter night after night, and all I had to do was ape his timing and inflections. The performance went by in a daze, but afterwards Renée Houston, a warm-hearted old trouper who had been quite a big name in her youthful vaudeville days, called me into her dressing room and congratulated me on the performance, declaring in her broad Scottish accent, with her large bosoms almost falling out of her negligée, "You'll be a star one day, laddie, mark my words."

Well, I suppose her forecast was optimistic, but it gave me great encouragement at the time.

Peter became a great friend, and took me out to dinner after the show at least once a week, to restaurants I could never afford on my ten pounds a week salary. He would talk enthusiastically about the theatre, about literature, about music – on all of which he seemed to my twenty year-old self astonishingly knowledgeable. He never married, in fact was almost certainly gay, but kept very discreet about it, especially in those far-off days when the practice was punishable with a jail sentence. But that was probably why he liked my company, although I was utterly naïve about such matters. He went on to have a distinguished career, playing the lead in the enjoyable TV series *Telford's Change*, and playing Edward VIII in the long-running play about the abdication, *Crown Matrimonial* by the wildly eccentric playwright, Royce Ryton (more later).

I stayed with the show for my first three month's contract period, tentatively experiencing the shadowy and exotic atmosphere of the London theatre world. But then my agent, John Penrose, said, "It's time you left there, and went into rep for some real acting experience."

John was a lascivious old queen, who picked up many of the promising young graduates from the drama schools who hadn't gone to more distinguished agents such as Al Parker and MCA. He had a reputation for being slightly shady, and for chasing pretty young boys around the desk. He had, however, very good connections with the repertory companies, which were numerous in those days, and was adept at finding places there for his clients.

He had seen me in my final performance at RADA, playing the wildly ambitious part of the general Melantius in the sub-Shakespearean epic, *The Maid's Tragedy* by Beaumont and Fletcher. Why he considered me worth representing, hidden as I was on stage behind a ferocious beard and hernia-inducing armour, I'm not sure, but I was extremely grateful for the offer, since graduating without an agent, as many students did, made an extremely inauspicious start to such a hazardous profession.

John did make some subtle advances in my direction, but soon realised that I was an incurable heterosexual, and settled instead for getting me employed as the 'juvenile lead' at Chesterfield Rep.

I went to Chesterfield in the winter of 1959, and found a rather dismal, and bitterly cold town, renowned only for its strangely twisted church spire, and its slightly tatty, but busily productive weekly repertory theatre. Once again I found myself in surroundings I did not find hospitable, and amongst company I was ill at ease with. They included my old class-mate at RADA, Edward Fox (eventually to gain stardom in *Day Of The Jackal)*, a ravishingly attractive blonde leading lady called Hal Dyer – with whom I was instantly infatuated, but had no hope whatsoever, already commandeered as she was by the leading man – and an intimidating character actress named Penelope Keith, built in the Edith Evans mould, who went on to a distinguished career as the star of such TV shows as *The Good Life* and *To The Manor Born*, and was indeed made a dame for her services to the arts and to charity.

However, I did not warm to the lady on first acquaintance, especially after having to make love to her in my first play there, the Terence Rattigan piece, *French Without Tears*, and after receiving various jibes from her waspish tongue.

Eddie Fox left soon after I joined, and in my loneliness at Chesterfield, I took up friendship with an older member of the company with whom I shared rather uncomfortable 'theatre digs' (such establishments abounded in most towns then, catering cheaply for the regular comings and goings of itinerant actors). He was called Godfrey Jackman, an ex-seaman, a man of many unconventional parts, an actor almost by accident, and gay. Godfrey took me under his wing, again with more hope than expectancy, and regaled me with colourful tales of the sea, and of his bizarre exploits around the world, before he fell by chance into the acting profession. He saved my sanity during those bleak months at Chesterfield, even though the rest of the company naturally assumed we were having a gay relationship – Miss Keith making such comments as, "Have fun – don't get arrested," as we left the theatre together after the show.

'Weekly' rep, now thankfully extinct, was, as its name implies, the business of mounting a production every week of the year, except for the pantomime season – which, being ever popular, ran for as many weeks as the management could achieve.

The process incredibly involved one having to be occupied with three different shows at one time – the play one was performing at night and for matinées, the play one was rehearsing during the day, ready for the following week, and the play after that, where one had to come to the first day's rehearsal at least vaguely familiar with the words if one was to have any hope of being coherent by the time it opened. The process meant that the company was embroiled in one text or the other from the moment they got up until the moment they went to bed. How anyone ever found time to eat, socialise, and have affairs in between, remains a mystery to me to this day. The standard of production must have been pretty appalling, since the best one could hope for was to step out onto the stage, surrounded by a rickety set on which the paint was still drying, with a vague knowledge of the correct order of words, but very little subtlety or characterisation.

It was some years before fortnightly rep became the norm, followed in the larger theatres by three-weekly productions. These were accompanied by a greatly improved standard of performance, but also by a rapid shrinkage in the number of repertory theatres. Which is a shame, because large parts of the population now no longer have immediate access to live theatre, but also because emerging actors no longer have access to the intense learning experience that such exposure to diverse parts provided.

My months at Chesterfield passed from winter into spring, and then I left, having implored John Penrose to find me something more amenable.

He obliged, and got me the leading juvenile part in *Tea and Sympathy,* at the much respected rep company in the wonderful historic city of York.

CHAPTER THREE

More Acting

My life was transformed.

Not only was it now springtime, with the cherry trees in full blossom around the ancient walls of the city; not only did I find myself in the most exotic digs any actor had ever discovered – on the attic floor of the grand National Trust mansion called The Treasurer's House, in the shadow of York Minster, surely one of the most magnificent of all the churches in Christendom; not only was I playing a leading part in one of the country's finest rep companies, set in one of the loveliest old theatres, the Theatre Royal; but I also embarked on my first real love affair.

Tea And Sympathy is a deeply moving play (previously staged and filmed, starring Deborah Kerr) about an affair between a sensitive teenage schoolboy and an unhappily married schoolmaster's wife. At York, the part of the wife was played by Veronica Strong, a flame-haired actress only a year older than myself, but well cast, being highly attractive in a more mature sort of way. Moved, partly perhaps by the influence of the story (an actor's frequent affliction), and partly by the sheer exuberance of our circumstances, Veronica and I fell in love.

The Theatre Royal company was run by an old actor/manager

called Donald Bodley, and included amongst others Alethea Charlton, June Barry, John Ronane, and Rodney Bewes (later one of *The Likely Lads*). They were a talented and enthusiastic bunch, and the atmosphere was wholly different to the inhospitable one at Chesterfield. During the run of the play, Donald Bodley asked me if I would like to stay on for the rest of the season as the 'juv lead' of the company. I was at first hesitant, being naively intent on speeding to West End stardom. However, being by now deeply involved with Veronica, and learning that the next production was to be an ambitious staging of both parts of Shakespeare's *Henry IV* (the plays featuring the glorious character of Falstaff), I consented, provided I could play the terrific part of Prince Hal, later Henry V.

Donald, somewhat critical of my arrogance, agreed. I then had the inspiring experience of working on perhaps the finest – certainly the most entertaining – of Shakespeare's history plays, rehearsing my speeches in the vast and appropriate medieval spaces of The Treasurer's House, exploring the equally evocative streets of that ancient city, and going home to the arms of my leading lady.

I did my Shakespearian best with Prince Hal, ever stirred by the splendidly engaging story of his tumultuous relationship with the fat old rogue Falstaff (which years later inspired me to compile into a book for a musical), and stayed for some six months at York, playing an assortment of parts, from young murderers in whodunnits, to dashing officers in wartime dramas, to incompetent singing/dancing roles in reviews.

Then one day, I received a long distance phone call from my agent, John Penrose, and my life changed again.

"I've got you an audition in London for a new play produced

by H.M. Tennent," he said. "You've just got time to catch the early morning train to King's Cross, get the tube to Piccadilly Circus, walk to the Globe Theatre in Shaftesbury Avenue, do the audition, and then catch the train back to York in time for the evening's performance. You'll find out more when you get there."

I duly did as instructed, knowing very little about the object of the audition. H.M. Tennent, headed by Hugh 'Binkie' Beaumont, were then the most prestigious and influential of West End producers, and their headquarters were at the Globe (now the Gielgud Theatre). When I arrived at the stage door, I joined a small queue of other hopefuls, and was handed two sheets of playscript, which told me little of what the piece was about, other than that my part was called Robin, an auspicious sign perhaps.

When my time came I walked hesitantly out onto the largest stage I had ever been on, peered into the blinding lights from the front, and waited. A grand upper-class voice called from the darkness, "Ah, Mr Hawdon, thank you for coming. You're going to read the part of Robin for us – yes?"

"Yes," I said.

"Good, good – well carry on. Diana there will read the other part with you. Just pretend she's an Arab prince." (This, I learned later, was Diana Boddington, bossy doyen of company managers.)

I duly read the short piece, was asked to read it again, and then was dismissed with the immortal words, "Thank you, we'll let you know," and left for the long journey back to York.

The following day John Penrose rang again, and said, "Congratulations – you've got the part."

"Oh," I said. "What is it?"

He exclaimed in astonishment, "Didn't they tell you?"

"No. Nothing."

"Well, hold on to your hat. It's a new play by Enid Bagnold" (a distinguished literary figure who had mingled with the famous Bloomsbury set, and who had recently had a big success with her play, *The Chalk Garden*, starring Dame Edith Evans and Peggy Ashcroft). "This is called *The Last Joke*, and it's starring Sir John Gielgud and Sir Ralph Richardson, Ernest Thesiger, Robert Flemyng, and a rising young actress called Anna Massey. It's to be directed by Glenn Byam Shaw (most illustrious of theatre directors), and you start rehearsals in a month, so give in your notice at York."

When I had picked myself off the floor, I staggered to the office of Donald Bodley, and explained the situation. I was still technically under contract to York rep, but Donald appreciated the chance I had been given, and gamely agreed to release me. At the age of twenty one I was headed back to the West End of London.

How do I describe the extraordinary experience of *The Last Joke*? The production was one of the last of the grand, baroque, stylised stagings that was rounding off the era of Noel Coward and Terence Rattigan and Jean Anouilh. The occasion was for me a mixture of awe-inspiring education, bewildering story telling, magisterial performing, farcical miscasting, and hugely entertaining off-stage episodes.

The piece itself was an incomprehensible (to me at any rate) tale of the clash of two gigantic egos – an art collecting billionaire, played by Richardson, and a Middle Eastern prince, played by Gielgud, hilariously sporting a fez and highly unconvincing accent.

The sets for the three separate acts were lavish and spectacular. The rehearsals were a riveting procedure of dramatic discussion and text argument between the three main participants – 'Johnny', 'Ralphy', and 'Glenny' – interrupted regularly by 'Eny' the authoress. My part was the not very large one of Ralph Richardson's personal valet, but at least it had one or two laugh lines in it. The entire production was misconceived, and slammed by most of the critics ('The last joke indeed!'). Gielgud's performance especially was branded the most miscast of his career.

And yet it seemed to my innocent young self that the whole marvellous business was surely what theatre, and the gods of theatre, were all about.

Several incidents stand out in my memory. One was of Anna Massey accepting an invitation one day after rehearsals, for a test drive on the back of the new and powerful motorbike just acquired by Ralph Richardson, who was addicted to fast transport of all kinds. She came back, shaking and white faced, and said, "We went round Regent's Park at eighty miles an hour!"

I thought she was probably exaggerating, until later one Saturday night, when the company was returning to London from its tour date at Blackpool. I had by now acquired my first car – an ancient Vauxhall Cresta – and was giving a lift to several others of the cast on the long drive back. Before we left the Grand Theatre at Blackpool, I had overheard Richardson saying to Gielgud, "Shall we have a spot of dinner before the drive, Johnny?" (The pair were long-standing friends and associates, having initiated various companies and productions together.)

Some three hours later, as we drove at the best speed my rickety old Vauxhall could achieve down what is now the M6 motorway, a stately Rolls Royce glided past at what must have been ninety miles an hour, with Sir Ralph at the wheel, and the two theatre knights chatting casually together on the front seats, having partaken of a good dinner, and no doubt a glass or two of wine.

Richardson was a true eccentric. He seemed to live in a world of his own. He never knew the names of anyone, bar close colleagues – always greeting me throughout the whole term of the production with "Hi, boy – how are you?"

He would rehearse by speaking the lines in his famously rasping voice, followed by audibly muttered stage directions to himself – "Close door, take off hat and gloves, sit at desk..." He did this right up to the dress rehearsal. And even during performances he could be seen still mouthing the commands. But he had an innate charm which shone through his persona, and made him the great character actor he was.

Gielgud was a quite different animal. Perhaps the most revered Shakespearian actor of the twentieth century, he was also known in those homophobic times for being a homosexual, largely because of his much-publicised trial for soliciting a few years previously. This had been a source of huge distress and embarrassment to him, and almost led to a nervous breakdown, even though the profession and most of the public cared little about it. The trial was one of the factors which led to the eventual decriminalising of the homosexual act between consenting adults.

Gielgud was descended from the distinguished Terry theatrical dynasty – his great aunt was Dame Ellen Terry, queen of the British theatre for decades over the turn of the century. And in the company of *The Last Joke* was another Terry, his cousin, Hazel Terry.

During the show I had to make an entrance with Sir John, holding the door open for him to march into Richardson's palatial drawing room, lined with old masters. I was usually waiting in the wings for this moment as Gielgud arrived, sporting heavy dark make-up and bright red fez, and he would greet me in that famous voice (described by Alec Guinness as 'a silver trumpet muffled in silk'). "Hello, Robin, how are you this evening?"

And I would give my deferential reply, "Fine, thank you, Sir John."

However, one night during our second week on tour, when we were playing the enormous Liverpool Empire, his greeting was different.

"Good evening, Robin. What are you doing after the show tonight?"

"Oh. Um – nothing, Sir John."

"Good. How would you like to have dinner at my hotel?"

Oh God, I thought – here we go again. However one can't turn down such an invitation from Sir John Gielgud. "Thank you, Sir John. I'd love to."

Then he twinkled at me, and murmured, "Don't worry. Hazel will be along too, to chaperone us."

The three of us walked to the Adelphi Hotel after the performance, and when we entered the grand circular dining room there, filled mostly with late diners who had been to see the play, a ripple of applause ran round the room. I basked a little in the glow, fearful also that I would immediately be seen as one of his *protégés*.

But it was a delightful evening – not only enlivened by the sort of gourmet dinner which I had rarely experienced, but also by the constant flow of theatre stories and quips that emanated from the great man's lips. He was renowned for making embarrassing *faux pas* (He once asked the then Prime Minister, Clement Attlee, at a dinner party, "Where are you living now?" eliciting the obvious answer, "Ten Downing Street"). But he made full use of the fact, turning the instances into hilarious anecdotes.

We toured the country for eight weeks, and ended up in London at the aforesaid Phoenix Theatre, for a thankfully brief run of only two months.

That was the start of a long period for me, living mostly in London, and now having to seriously embrace the actor's uncertain life of waiting for phone calls from agents or producers.

However, as always, I had my writing to fall back on.

CHAPTER FOUR

Writing

Over the next few years I was rarely out of work as an actor. A hazy succession of parts – some minor, some major – in rep, in the West End, in TV, and in the occasional film, the order of which I can scarcely recollect. I longed to excel in musicals, and spent money I could ill afford on singing lessons from a well-known German opera coach called Alfred Kuhn (my favourite TV event to this day is the original Three Tenors concert, which exploded onto our screens like all the Promenade Concerts rolled into one).

I even auditioned for the part of Freddie in *My Fair Lady*, attempting his signature song, '*On The Street Where You Live*.' But eventually the producers, and Alfred Kuhn, and especially myself, had to accept that I would never make a singer.

However at the same time I was always scribbling. Scribbling in the Notting Hill flat I now shared with Veronica (who had also returned to London), in dressing rooms and rehearsal spaces whilst waiting for my next entrance, in cafés and bars, in digs and hotels, on trains and planes. Sheaves and sheaves of paper (this was of course long before the glorious advent of the word-processor), covered with scrawls and erasings and inserts, most of which ended up in the waste bin.

I had actually written my first play whilst at RADA. It was a thinly disguised family drama inspired all too obviously by the immensely moving *Five Finger Exercise*, first West End play by Peter Shaffer – to my mind the finest playwright of the late twentieth century, whatever the critics say about Harold Pinter, whose obscure pieces I never really identified with.

Mine was titled *Gods and Goddesses*, was extremely convoluted and pretentious, and languishes still in a dark drawer somewhere. It was however the beginnings of a learning process that continues to this day.

My next effort was more successful – an all male confrontation between a professor, an artist, a politician, and a labourer, trapped together in a rustic barn – and titled *Barn Dance*. It was supposed to be a satire on the four competing elements of human nature, cloaked in the guise of a comic encounter. It was produced at the Hampstead Theatre Club, perhaps the pre-eminent London fringe theatre to this day. I was extremely pleased with the casting, and with the impressive, heavy-beamed design of the set, which had to collapse around the actors' ears at the end of the play (symbolic, or what?). The reviews were mixed, but not disastrous, and I felt I could now call myself a playwright.

My next effort was more successful, still more philosophical, and even more bizarre. It was partly inspired by Samuel Beckett's immortal piece, *Waiting For Godot*, which had exploded on the London scene some years previously. Lost for a theme for another play, I wondered what would happen if I set two characters on stage, with no names, no background, no setting – in fact nothing at all to characterise them – and let them start to discover life and the universe from scratch. It was titled *The Secret*, and first produced at the Kings Lynn Festival, directed by Braham Murray, and received one or two rave reviews, and one or two bewildered ones. I assumed that would be the end of it, but then, astonishingly, my newly acquired literary agent at London Management sold it to a producer looking for something *avant garde* to mount at the illustrious Salzburg Festival in Austria.

Thus began another of my remarkable out-of-the-blue experiences in the theatre business. I was invited to go to Austria, all expenses paid, and attend rehearsals.

The Festival Theatre at Salzburg is an imposing building in the centre of that most picturesque of towns, surrounded by the lakes and mountains of the Northern Alps. The Festival itself is mostly founded on musical events, but, like many others, intersperses these with theatrical ones. I was to visit it again years later in totally different, but just as extraordinary circumstances.

My play was directed by a respected German director, Harry Mayen, starred four well-known German/Austrian actors, and displayed a set which exceeded anything my imagination could have conceived. The setting was required to display the gradual revelation from nothing, of a vast panorama of sky, mountains and forests – a daunting task for a designer. At Salzburg it was achieved by phasing in the lighting behind a huge blank gauze cyclorama, on a spectacular backdrop with realistic solid trees soaring in front of it.

I had little to do during rehearsals, having been banished to the back of the stalls by the director, who wasn't interested in my twenty four year-old observations. However, his then fiancée was the gorgeous actress, Romy Schneider – star of many Hollywood and Continental pictures – who also came to watch a lot of the rehearsals for want of anything better to do. She and I spent much of the time whispering together in the darkness of the big theatre. She was older than me, and not remotely interested in me as a sexual object, in complete contrast to myself, but at least it enlivened the proceedings.

The Director of the Festival came to see a dress rehearsal, and afterwards proclaimed that the play would become 'a great classic of modern theatre'. However, most of the critics disagreed, and it vanished after its run, never to be heard of again.

I then decided it was time I stopped experimenting with the surreal stuff, and wrote something more relevant. The result, some years later, was *The Hero*. A ridiculously ambitious piece about a power-hungry Churchillian politician, whose scheming methods led to a crisis in British politics. Its theme was the ever present one famously described by Lord Acton, that 'all power corrupts, and absolute power corrupts absolutely'.

This grandiose literary effort led to one of the most stressful, but intriguing periods of my life. During the year or more of the writing, I had serious need of informed advice on political matters. I managed somehow to get interviews with Chapman Pincher, the pre-eminent Fleet Street political reporter at the time, and with Anthony Wedgewood Benn ('Tony Benn') the left-wing Minister for Technology – both of whom were extremely cooperative, and gave me useful information, much of which I have long forgotten.

However, what I really needed was first-hand knowledge of how cabinet meetings were conducted within 10 Downing Street. Not just the procedural details, but the actual confidential interchanges between Prime Ministers and their coterie. I pondered much about who to approach for such information. Then someone said, "Well, you may as well start at the top, and with someone who is retired and has the time. Why not write to Harold Macmillan?"

Macmillan had recently resigned as Prime Minister, finally brought down, as politicians invariably are, by the caprices of fate – in his case illness, and the Profumo scandal. He was known as 'Supermac' and the 'Last of the great Edwardians' with the reputation of being gracious, diplomatic, and Machiavellian. I at first rejected the idea as being ludicrously presumptuous, but then, in desperation, sent a letter addressed to him at Macmillan's the publishers, his family firm, with very little expectation of a reply.

Astonishingly, I shortly received a letter from his secretary, stating that Mr Macmillan (not yet the Earl of Stockton) was intrigued by the premise of my play, and would like to invite me to lunch at his home to discuss it. I was given a possible date several weeks ahead, and of course accepted.

On the appointed day, I followed precise instructions and drove nervously down to his address, Birch Grove, in Sussex. I entered the huge iron gates to find an imposing Queen Anne mansion set within lovely gardens, and surrounded by rolling wooded hills. There was no one in sight, except for an old gardener pottering amongst the flower beds, so I parked the car and walked up the steps to the large front door. Whilst I was searching for the right knocker or bell to use, I heard shuffling footsteps behind me, and turned to see the gardener approaching across the gravel. I then realised that

I had made my first blunder, and that this was in fact the ex-Prime Minister himself, clad in old clothes and galoshes.

"Can I help you?" he asked in his instantly recognisable, old Etonian accent.

"Um – I've come for lunch, sir. To talk about my play."

"Good heavens! You're the playwright chappie. Bit young to be doing that, aren't you?" (I always looked youthful for my age, and some would say stayed immature always.)

He went on, "Well, tell you what – it's a lovely day, let's go for a walk in the garden before we have lunch."

We duly wandered around the large, immaculately manicured gardens, whilst he regaled me with stories about past and present politicians, brought to mind by my play. His memory was astonishing. Not only could he recall debates between, say, Gladstone and Disraeli, but also the actual dates and places where they occurred. He only broke off to contemplate a bed of roses, which he said had been planted by his wife, Lady Dorothy, daughter of the Duke of Devonshire, who had died fairly recently. "I miss her," he said sadly, despite the fact that, as I knew, the marriage had been blighted by her life-long affair with Lord Boothby, another Tory grandee. The amorous conducts of the upper classes rivalled even those of the stars, and probably still do.

We then stopped at the edge of the garden and looked out over a magnificent vista of many acres of Sussex forest land.

"What a lovely view," I exclaimed.

"Yes," he said. And added, "It's all mine." Sigh. "Don't know what I'm going to do with it all." (The family was immensely wealthy after the growth of the global Macmillan publishing business.)

We then returned to the house for a three course lunch, just the two of us sitting at one end of a huge mahogany dining table – which must have seen many far more distinguished occasions in the past – served by a white-gloved manservant. Macmillan himself ate little, but spent the time regaling me with fascinating insights into the devious ways of inner government wheeling-and-dealing, and virtually rewriting the play for me.

After lunch he took me to see the large office built over his stable block, where no less than three secretaries were typing away at letters and the memoirs he was currently writing – all from the shorthand text he had previously dictated to them, entirely from memory.

I left with my head spinning with ideas and information, and drove back to London, scarcely concentrating on the road.

I had by now moved both my acting and writing activities to the agency of Richard Stone, a long established and greatly resourceful agent (unlike some), with whom I stayed for over twenty years until his personal retirement from the firm he founded. Dear Richard tried to get various London producers interested in *The Hero*, but without success.

However I then sent it to a director I knew vaguely through certain awkward discords over his then girlfriend (don't ask). This was Peter Coe, director of such successful musicals as *Lock Up Your Daughters*, *Oliver* and *Kiss Me Kate*.

Peter rang me up, and, graciously forgiving previous frictions, said, "I like this. I think we could do something with it." With him on board, we were able to interest the impresario, Henry Sherwood. We then set about the problem of casting (forever the writer's and producer's greatest challenge). For the daunting central role various star names were approached, but all were either unavailable or not interested. I was keen on the idea of Harry Andrews, the tall, granite-jawed, sergeant-major figure of countless British war films. He had just the right formidable presence for the role, and professed to want to come back to the stage. He read the play, and got very enthusiastic about it, inviting me to his lovely country house to discuss it. He was in real life the antithesis of his public persona – charming, soft-spoken, and gay – and we talked at length about the possibilities. However, once again my hopes were dashed when he was offered another far more lucrative film deal, and regretfully turned me down.

Then Peter Coe said, "How about Roy Dotrice? I know him, and he's looking for a play."

Roy wasn't quite my idea of the character, being rather slight and debonair, but he was a fine actor, and now a big name after a long West End run with his hilarious one-man show *Brief Lives*, in which he portrayed the doddering 17th century diarist, John Aubrey.

Roy read and accepted the part, and was joined in the large cast by other well-known faces such as Robert Harris and Elizabeth Sellars. It also had a walk-on part for a stunningly beautiful coloured girl named Shakira Baksh, who later became Michael Caine's lifelong wife.

I felt that my ambitions to be a recognised serious playwright were coming to fruition.

But then the trials began.

It soon transpired during the rehearsal period that Peter Coe had a rather different vision for the production to my own. I intended the play to be set within the imposing historical surroundings of Westminster and Parliament. Peter wanted to modernise it, and commissioned a rather bare set surrounded by banks of distracting television screens. Furthermore, he wanted the minor role of the central character's mistress to be played completely in the nude, which I felt was gratuitous. Then, to cap it all, he decided that the piece should be a thinly veiled portrayal of Enoch Powell, the brilliant, but hugely contentious MP of the time, who had just been sacked from the Shadow Cabinet by Edward Heath after his notorious 'Rivers of Blood' speech.

I fought strongly against this development, feeling that the play should not be about any specific contemporary figure, which would immediately make it the object of irrelevant and distracting debate.

Our arguments went on throughout rehearsals, until I was forced to leave the company to it during the final week, for fear of disrupting things too much. However, when I went to see the first dress rehearsal at Edinburgh, our opening tour date, I discovered to my dismay that Peter had inserted his own long and wordy scene between members of the fictional Cabinet, which was both tedious and quite unrelated to the play's theme. The rehearsal was followed by a terrible late-night confrontation in Roy Dotrice's hotel room, during which Peter and I shouted at each other, with Roy, torn between us both and almost in tears, trying to keep the peace.

I was still young, and fairly inexperienced in the ways of theatre diplomacy, and handled the situation badly, especially as I was intimidated by Peter Coe's distinguished reputation and aloof personality. However the producer, by now fully aware of the situation, agreed over various long distance phone calls, that he would not bring the play into London unless I was completely happy with it.

Needless to say, I wasn't, and the production folded after its final tour date. It was the first of several disappointments throughout my career.

However, it resulted in a fascinating later commission, of which more later.

CHAPTER FIVE

More Writing

Some while before the episode of *The Hero*, I had written another play. Something completely different to everything else hitherto. In a moment of naïve optimism I had thought to myself, 'It's time I made some real money at this writing business. I'll knock off a quick comedy. It can't be difficult.'

Light 'boulevard' comedies and farces were the mainstay of the commercial theatre at that time. This was well before the pandemic of musicals swamped every stage just large enough to accommodate them. Hardly a week went by in those golden days when some new comedy by William Douglas Home, Hugh and Margaret Williams, Peter Ustinov, Neil Simon, Alan Ayckbourn, Leslie Storm, Terence Frisby, Keith Waterhouse, et al, was not opening, and invariably playing to packed houses whatever the critics had to say, simply because of the star power they were able to attract. Major names such as Ian Carmichael, Kenneth More, Alastair Sim, Rex Harrison, Moira Lister, Robert Morley, Margaret Rutherford, Richard Briers, Joan Greenwood, Donald Sinden, Leslie Phillips, Phyllis Calvert, and David Tomlinson, were happy to do at least a six month stint making fools of themselves in some frothy light-hearted piece. Even distinguished classical thesps like Sir Ralph Richardson and

Dame Peggy Ashcroft could occasionally be persuaded to dabble in the genre, and ageing film stars such as Stewart Granger, Margaret Lockwood and Glynis Johns were sometimes tempted back to the boards, with varying results. And of course, down the road from Trafalgar Square, Brian Rix was dropping his trousers nightly at the Whitehall Theatre, to gales of laughter in speed-of-light-so-you-don't-see-the-joins farces by Ray Cooney and John Chapman.

I decided to contribute to the lucrative form.

I could not know that this insouciant decision was to radically affect the rest of my life – in both a beneficial and a negative way. Beneficial because it eventually brought a more-or-less steady income which continues to this day. Negative because it branded me as a lightweight playwright whose attempts at real drama were not worth serious consideration.

It also put me on another learning curve – this time lasting for eight years.

After some thought, I came up with an idea for such a piece. My first draft turned out to be about four hours long. So I rewrote it. The next effort was three hours long. I rewrote it. I was learning the truth of Dr Johnson's axiom, 'Brevity is the soul of wit'. I finally got it down to two hours, and sent it off to all the producers I could think of. No one was interested. I put it away in a drawer and forgot about it.

Then, a year or so later, I went to see the hit comedy, *There's A Girl In My Soup,* by Terence Frisby, and starring Donald Sinden and Barbara Ferris. It was a delightful evening, and sent me out of the theatre thinking, 'There's a laugh almost every other line in that play. I wonder whether mine is as funny?'

I dug out my old script and re-read it. Of course it wasn't. I began the exhausting process of trying to make every line and every incident *funny.*

Those who have never attempted such a feat have no idea how difficult it is. They watch the popular plays and TV shows, and assume that the torrent of laugh lines just roll off the writer's pen with the ease of a stream flowing downhill. In fact, it is a tortuous process of thinking, 'I can't just write, "Good night, see you tomorrow." It has to be a laugh line.' Or, 'This character can't simply pour a whiskey – it has to be turned into a joke.'

I am always in awe of the long-running American TV shows such as *Friends, Frazier*, and *Seinfeld*, where, even after several hundred episodes, the authors still manage to maintain a constant flow of witty situations and dialogue. But of course, those are all written by committees of writers, clustered round a table and throwing ideas at each other. The British classics, such as *Fawlty Towers* and *Yes Minister* only ran for a limited number of episodes, before the individual writers wisely called a stop out of sheer inventive fatigue.

The other major lesson of comedy writing is that the fun doesn't really come from clever lines. It comes from *character.* We roar at Basil Fawlty because his utter lack of control over his own fury at the tricks of fate mirrors what we all feel.

I am not an instinctively witty person. I slaved at my script for several months before I got it into what I felt was a more feasible comedy play. And I sent it off again.

Remarkably, the response I got was almost immediate. I received a phone call one evening, and a rather grand theatrical voice said,

"This is Peter Saunders. I've read your play. It's very funny. I'd like to produce it."

Peter Saunders (later Sir Peter) was one of the most successful of West End impresarios. His major achievement was the mounting of Agatha Christie's *The Mousetrap*, which became the world's longest running production (currently as I write, in its sixty eighth year in London), and which enabled him to freely experiment with many other shows. He invited me to lunch at The Ivy (famous show biz restaurant) to discuss mine. I enjoyed another lavish meal at someone else's expense, and spent an agreeable couple of hours in Peter's genial company, gaily discussing tour dates, and West End theatres, and tossing star names around like confetti.

However, it wasn't of course that easy. As ever, the big box office names were all either already committed, or much in demand by everyone else. After six months of trying, Peter said to me, "I'll tell you what we'll do. We'll put it on at Bromley with as good a cast as we can get, and see how it goes, and get people to come down and see it."

Bromley was one of the half dozen 'try-out' repertory theatres ringing the capital, along with Guildford, Windsor, Watford, etc, which were all happy to co-produce shows with London producers, sharing the costs, and knowing they would probably pull in the local audiences.

Peter, and Bromley's director, David Poulson, mounted the play, then titled *As Long As It's Warm*, with the quite young, but already established personality, Nicholas Parsons, contracted to play the lead, and my first love, Veronica, who I was no longer living with (more later), also in the cast.

Then fate struck again. David Poulson rang me one morning, a week before we were due to open, and said, "Nicholas Parsons has gone down with mumps, and can't continue."

I was naturally distraught. But in fact it turned out to be one of the luckiest accidents of my career. David then said, "The only thing I can think of, is to ring Ray Cooney and see if he'll do it. Ray's always up for anything."

Ray Cooney was, and still is, probably the most successful farce writer the British theatre has ever produced. His outrageously implausible concoctions kept Brian Rix and his company busy at the Whitehall Theatre, tearing round the stage, losing trousers, skirts, dignities and sanities, to the delight of audiences, year in, year out.

Ray was also a very funny actor himself, in the same frantic, strangle-voiced style of that company at the time.

David tracked him down on holiday with his family, on Jersey of all places, told him the story, and dear Ray, without even seeing the script, promptly agreed to abandon his loved ones in the midst of their summer vacation, and flew back to take over the part with less than a week's rehearsal. I suspect he was bored with the inactivity of a beach holiday, and welcomed the opportunity.

The first night at Bromley seemed to me to be a big success. Ray and the cast worked their socks off, all the onstage gadgetry, which was a major feature of the piece, worked on time, and the audience roared satisfactorily in most of the right places. I thought I had finally done it.

However, then came another of those unexpected blows that show business delights in dealing. Peter Saunders came to me after the curtain came down, and said, "I don't know what to do with this play. I thought it was a charming light comedy, but it's actually an outright farce. I'm afraid it's not for me."

He was right of course. Ray's instinctive style had turned the play into a much more farcical experience than I had intended, but it was probably all the funnier for that.

I was naturally dismayed, and ready to abandon all thoughts of being a comic playwright.

Then, some days later, Ray rang me himself. "Robin, I gather that Peter doesn't wish to take up his option on the play."

"Yes, that's right."

"Well, I think we can do a lot with it. We need to work on it, and tighten up the dialogue, but I'd like to take up the option."

Ray had himself begun to dally with producing (he later founded the huge project of the Theatre of Comedy, based at the Shaftesbury Theatre, and involving all the top comedy names in the business). Thus began what turned out to be several more years of try-outs, summer seasons, tours (in one of which I acted myself, not very successfully), and rewritings, and more rewritings, before the play, now titled, *The Mating Game*, and starring the comedian Terry Scott, Aimi MacDonald, Clive Francis, Julia Lockwood and Avril Angers, finally made it to the West End for a long run at the Apollo Theatre. The whole process, from the moment I gaily thought 'I'll knock off a quick comedy', to the first night in London, had taken about eight years.

I read *The Mating Game* text now, and wince at its naivety. It attracted lukewarm notices after its premiere, although most acknowledged that the audience found it hilarious. It went on to regularly tour the land, starring such names as David Jason, Barbara Windsor, Peggy Mount, Norman Vaughan, and even a previous Miss World, and to play in over thirty different countries, bringing me an income for many decades.

It was followed by a number of other, more sophisticated comedies, none quite so successful as the genre declined in London, but all finding regular productions around the country and abroad, and culminating in the success of *Don't Dress For Dinner*, which deserves a chapter all on its own.

CHAPTER SIX

Acting and Romancing

The years between *The Last Joke* and the London run of *The Mating Game* were filled with a fairly constant procession of acting jobs, many of which I scarcely recollect, but some of which stand out in my memory.

In films I played minor roles as Dirk Bogarde's student, Richard Todd's son (forcing him to stand on a box for our close-shots, as he was not very tall), Vanessa Redgrave's admirer, Dudley Moore's rival for the hand of Eleanor Bron in *Bedazzled*, in which I had the distasteful job of sucking her big toe. I also played sidekick to Vivien Leigh's gigolo, Warren Beatty, in his first starring movie, and her final one, *The Roman Spring of Mrs Stone*. Most of my part ended up on the cutting room floor, but it was intriguing to meet the legendary star of *Gone With The Wind*, still radiating seductive blue eyes, and also the exotic looking Beatty (brother of Shirley MacLaine), who came with an already notorious Hollywood reputation.

On television, I again played several parts early on, in a number of TV plays and series, one of which involved me actually having to out-camp Frankie Howerd in an episode of *The Frankie Howerd Show*. The star surprisingly let me get away with it.

My most notable TV employment was probably a year's stint in one of the early 'soaps'. This was *Compact*, a long-running twice weekly BBC show, which actually went out live. A frightening experience when first encountered, since one knew there was no help if one dried, except from the quick wits of one's fellow actors. However, the old stagers in the cast were used to it, and actually played tricks on newcomers such as myself, in the hopes of making them 'corpse' on air. I soon joined their ranks.

The show was built around the staff of a woman's magazine, and involved the newsroom journalists and various visiting characters connected with breaking news stories. I played a reporter called Barry Southern, and for the first and last time in my career found myself the object of fan worship from teenage school girls. There was an embarrassing incident when, on a day off, I went with a girlfriend to Stratford-on-Avon to see a Royal Shakespeare Company production, and was assaulted by a horde of uniformed teenagers emerging from several coaches, all shrieking and demanding autographs. The show was held up for several moments as the foyer was cleared of the throng, but then in the interval the same thing happened, and I had to escape into the gents toilet. Older members of the audience were heard demanding, "Who *is* that?" Not surprising in a theatre producing the world's greatest playwright, and employing some of the most distinguished thespians in the land.

I left *Compact* after a year, seeking more artistic employment, unlike many of the cast who, more practically-minded, stayed with it for several years, and set themselves up financially for long into the future. However, I had been earning the princely sum of £100 a week, a large sum for me then, and had a bit in the bank. I had also learned to play poker during those heady days, it being a popular pastime for cast members waiting for their next scene in the episodic show. For a long time after that I hosted a weekly poker game at home for a number of like-minded theatre people, including film star Stanley Baker, and Richard Wilson (Victor Meldrew in TV's *One Foot In The Grave).*

However, having taken the gamble of leaving such secure employment, I had to cut back on the expenditure and seek further work. I went back to the stage. In no particular order, I performed at Bristol Old Vic in a romantic Anouilh play, *The Fighting Cock.* At the Newbury Watermill Theatre I did James Saunders great play, *Bodies.* At Cheltenham I had the lead in John Mortimer's finest piece, *A Voyage Round My Father.* At Guildford, I played Lysander in *A Midsummer Night's Dream,* Billy in *Billy Liar* (an actor's dream part), St Francis of Assisi(!) in *The Door*, and the lead in a splendidly theatrical thriller titled *Ghost Train* by Arnold Ridley, whom many will remember as the doddery old Private Godfrey in TV's *Dad's Army.* This play had been a regular on the provincial circuits since its 1925 London production, and Arnold, himself playing the old Station Master in this production, told me that, as a hard-up novice playwright, he had sold the worldwide rights to the original producer for £200, which mistake he calculated had lost him several hundred thousand in future royalties.

During one of the hottest summers on record, I did a tour of the splendid J.B. Priestly play, *Time And The Conways*, starring Dulcie Gray, and directed by her husband, Michael Denison – a hilariously argumentative combination. In it the cast had to age twenty years between the acts. I played another major character called Robin. Priestly himself, an old man now, came to see us, and said to me in a quavering Yorkshire voice, "You're the best Robin I've ever seen." A rare compliment.

I also played in London as the Aviator in Shaw's *Misalliance* with Barbara Jefford (missing an entrance on the first night!); in *Not In The Book,* as Wilfred Hyde White's son; and as Algernon in *The Importance of Being Earnest,* with Neil Stacey, and my old RADA friend, Amanda Grinling.

Ironically, both Neil and Amanda later became near neighbours after we had moved to Bath – Neil living in aristocratic splendour in a National Trust apartment in Dyrham Park, once seat of the Blathwayt family – and Amanda, now married to Simon Relph, the film producer, in a lovely period house outside the city, where Simon created a prize-winning garden. Also, Veronica, my first love, and her husband Jeremy Burnham, came to live close by, followed by my old flat mate, Derek Fowlds, at whose first wedding I had been best man. We were a Bath community of old associates. But all that came much later.

My longest spell in the West End was six months at the Duke of York's theatre, singing(?), dancing, and generally fooling about, in the review, *One Over The Eight,* starring Kenneth Williams and a somewhat aloof Sheila Hancock.

Kenneth Williams was an extraordinary character. As outrageously camp in real life as he was in all his multifarious appearances on TV, radio, and the *Carry On* films, he was, underneath, a highly intelligent and well-read, but disturbed creature. He cloaked his sexual inadequacy with a constant flow of bawdy jokes and pranks, frequently exposing himself flippantly to girls in the show, and actually coming on stage for the dress rehearsal of the final number, stark naked except for a swept-back dressing gown. Then, when the cast collapsed in laughter, he loudly berating them for not continuing with the show. Today, the women would no doubt have had him prosecuted, but then they all took it in their stride.

He and Peter Cook, the writer of the review, would spar endlessly together, occasionally joined by Dudley Moore when he visited, all trying to outdo each other with funny voices and exaggerated stories. I wish I'd had a video camera.

Kenneth didn't drive, and on the pre-London tour I had given him and comedian Lance Percival, another member of the cast, a lift to the provincial date in my old Vauxhall. As we drove past a church on a rainy afternoon, a wedding limousine with bride and groom on board, pulled out and skidded straight into my car. In the ensuing furore of accusations, bride's tears, and police sirens, Kenneth, not concerned with the poor bride's situation, nor with the damage to my car, went into paroxysms of terror at the publicity it might attract for himself. I was only surprised that he didn't turn it into another comedy sketch for the benefit of all the onlookers.

After that I landed the title role at Birmingham rep in a play named *The Easter Man,* by the distinguished American writer, Evan Hunter (author of screenplays *The Blackboard Jungle* and Hitchcock's *The Birds,* and also of all the Ed McBain detective books). This was a piece about four young Americans meeting up for a wild weekend at an apartment in New York, and required American accents. Joining me in the cast were Ian McShane, Suzan

Farmer, and Karin Fernald, daughter of John Fernald my old RADA principle. Ian and I didn't really get on, two young stags in the rutting season, but the play was sufficiently successful for it to come to London and play the Globe theatre for several weeks – filling in, I suspect, before the management could find something more starry. The London notices were good, and remarkable for giving Karin Fernald especially the accolades one dreams about – 'A star is born!', 'A new young actress lights up the stage!'. She went on to a lengthy career, mostly as solo performer and speaker, but never quite fulfilling those early tributes.

By now the Swinging Sixties were well into their stride, not that we recognised them as anything different at the time. The Beatles and the Rolling Stones were filling the stadiums and airways, Mary Quant mini-skirts were swaying down the Kings Road, films such as *Darling, The Knack, and Alfie* were depicting the sexual freedoms, and on stage, shows such as *Hair* and *Oh Calcutta!* were heading to town to shock audiences with their outright nudity and profanity (one memorable line in *Hair,* long before today's ubiquitous use, was "Oh fuck! Oh fucky, fucky, fuck-fuck-fuck!").

London night life was booming, with theatre and arty people letting their long hair down at Gerry's Club, The Arts, and Tramp's; posh people at Annabel's and The Pheasantry; jazz enthusiasts at Ronnie Scott's, Chris Barber's and Humphrey Lyttleton's; and satire fans at The Establishment.

I was never a great night club goer – not quite understanding why anyone would wish to bankrupt themselves getting drunk in a dark cellar, where you could neither see who you were dancing with, nor hear what they were saying. However I did enjoy the general convivial and erotic spirit of the times. I remember an occasion when I was with a current girlfriend, actress Jill Curzon, having tea at the Dorchester – a trendy thing to do at the time, I can't think why. A couple came to sit at the next table, only a few yards away. We realised that they were Richard Burton and Elizabeth Taylor, evidently in one of their married or reconciliation phases. They were deep in conversation (probably discussing the terms of their next divorce). I suggested to the very attractive Jill that she walk past them on her way to the ladies, while I watched to see if Burton clocked her. She duly did so, and he duly did – giving her a long appreciative stare, both front and back. Then, when she returned, he did the same. So Jill suggested I repeat the stunt to see whether Liz Taylor noticed me. I did so, but when I came back, Jill just shook her head. "Not a glance."

A similar thing happened when I got into a lift at the BBC, at the same time as a pretty production assistant, to find Natalie Wood and husband Robert Wagner facing us. They both acknowledged our startled looks, but then Natalie Wood (ever one of my most idolised icons) studiously ignored me, whilst hubby Wagner continued to ogle the girl next to me. Perhaps it's the difference between the sexes.

Sexual exploration was everywhere – probably as it had always been, but now out in the open. Girls, liberated by the pill, were free to admit their sexuality as much as men, and there was none of the prurient, anti-male attitudes that prevails today. In fact a woman would be offended if she *didn't* get wolf-whistled at by the builders up on the scaffolds.

And as always, amongst the show business fraternity, sex proliferated probably more than anywhere else. Many plays, and certainly most films, embraced it as a major component, and of course still do. Film stars are chosen because of their sex appeal as much as their acting ability. It doesn't matter whether the movie is a thriller, a political drama, or a romantic comedy – if a Cary Grant, or Robert Redford, or George Clooney, or Brad Pitt – never mind the host of beautiful female names – is in it, the box office receipts will be fairly secure. Therefore the whole industry is subconsciously infected with the sexual imperative, and everyone involved in it responds.

I was always amused, when reaching a distant location for a film or TV production, to see the crew, made up mostly of grizzled veteran electricians, props guys, and camera-men, disappearing in buses and taxis the moment their plane or train arrived. When I first asked where they were all going, the production manager twinkled at me and said, "To the brothels of course. They always know where the best ones are."

And amongst the actors it was rife. Rep companies, touring casts, TV or film productions, were ever the centre of prolific flirtations, romances, and rivalries. The off-stage and off-set activities challenged anything the fiction writers could invent. And around the casts, a host of fringe hangers-on – models, extras, stunt people, production assistants, and all – joined in the fun.

I once went to a large Miss World Contest party, where the girls were all the national beauty contest winners, and the male contingent was mostly made up of journalists, agents, and publicity people – and as far as I could tell, none of the lovely contestants left the bash unescorted for the night.

As Dudley Moore said, "All I'm interested in is a lot of meaningful one-night stands."

Of course it is the reason why so many show business marriages don't last.

I won't go into detail, but naturally, liberated at last from my inhibiting upbringing and school days, I took full advantage of the situation.

I was never a wildly promiscuous participant. I have never visited a brothel for instance. But I was always on the lookout for love, for involvement, as well as for the perfect body. Veronica and I had reluctantly broken up after a year of living together, but I knew that, only twenty two (going on sixteen) as I was then, it would have been madness to make a lifelong commitment. She and I went our separate ways, and much later both found marriage within a year or two of each other. We are still good friends.

CHAPTER SEVEN

Marriage and Property

I was twenty eight, still awaiting the West End production of *The Mating Game*, and recently finishing another year-long love affair with the lovely sister-in-law of one of my best friends, distinguished documentary producer, Mischa Scorer.

I had for some years been sharing a large flat on the sprawling top-floor of a big Victorian house in Barnes, owned by an eccentric Irish professor and his family, who loved the theatre, and held riotous drunken parties downstairs for us and many others whenever the chance arose. It was my first sight of baths filled with ice and champagne bottles. I have been addicted to the great French tipple ever since.

In the flat below us lived the National Theatre director, John Dexter, and his boyfriend, a member of the *West Side Story* cast. The latter taught us all how to do the Twist and the Shake, the trendy dances of the day. One of the landlord's close friends was Paco Pena, the world famous Spanish guitarist, and whenever he was in the country he would join the parties, and add to the musicality of the evening by playing his guitar, accompanied erratically by the host on his Irish fiddle.

I shared the apartment with a number of other mates from the

RADA days, who came and went as their careers dictated. These included Peter Tory, my closest friend from drama school (whose greatest claim to fame was an affair with Julie Christie whilst on a Royal Shakespeare Company tour. He then left acting for journalism, and rose to become one of Fleet Street's best known gossip columnists.) Also his brother David – a computer whizz who went on to become the wealthy CEO of a hi-tec company in America; Derek Fowlds – soon to become well known as PPS Bernard in TV's *Yes Minister*; Ian Lindsay – the fussy office manager in *Men Behaving Badly*; and several others who slept on whichever bed, sofa, or floor space was available. All these were accompanied over the years by various interchanging wives, mistresses, casual girlfriends, and hangers-on, the dynamics of which were far too complicated to describe here.

One day in midsummer, several of us were sitting on the terrace of a Chelsea pub, often frequented by show-biz people, when we noticed a couple close by who were also talking theatre. We all got chatting, and they joined us at our table. The man was a struggling fellow actor, and the girl was a very pretty blonde who I was instantly drawn to. She sat opposite me, next to Peter Tory, and paid him far more attention than myself (she later said I looked too much like trouble – whatever that implied).

I, however, was seriously smitten, and, having learned that her partner that day was just a gay friend, and also who her agent was, played a seriously unprofessional card by ringing the latter the following day. I declared that I was working on the casting for *The Mating Game,* and thought his client could be right for the girl in the play. Might I perhaps have her phone number, so that I could meet and talk with her? Rather to my surprise, and contrary to all the ethics of the business, he consented and gave me the vital number.

Her name was Sheila Davies, a graduate of the Guildhall drama school, and a mere twenty one years old. I rang and asked her out. She was too startled to say no.

Our first two dates were to the theatre to see the rising star Pauline Collins lighting up the stage in a play called *The Happy Apple* at the Hampstead Theatre, followed by Jimmy Edwards and Eric Sykes in a hilariously shambolic farce titled *Big Bad Mouse*.

I had by now bought myself a second-hand but much sleeker version of my Vauxhall Cresta – this one being large and black, with tinted windows and whitewall tyres, and known by all my friends as my gangster car. It enabled me to drive one-handed, with my arm round the latest girlfriend, snuggled up on the red leather upholstery of the front bench seat.

Sheila said it merely confirmed her suspicions that I was 'trouble', but consented to drive to the Malvern Hills for a romantic weekend at the house of a friend, and our fates were sealed. She ever afterwards proclaimed that she didn't get the part in my play, she got me instead, but was never sure which would have been the better deal.

We got married some six months later in the charming small Welsh town of Montgomery, where Sheila's parents farmed a large dairy farm on the Earl of Powis's estate. My family and all my old friends from London came to the wedding, which was held in the rather splendid parish church, and the whole village came out to witness the rare spectacle of a posse of London actors parading down the main street in their hired wedding tails, to the reception at a local country house hotel.

Thus began a marriage which has lasted through inevitable ups and downs (the occasional Hawdon family rows could be as dramatic as anything on stage), but always with love, through over fifty years. Considering that it was a show business marriage, and that my own parents had fairly fractured marital histories, that is some achievement. The union brought us two stunning daughters, four equally stunning grandchildren, homes in four different countries, various differing careers for both of us, and a bevy of friends from all walks of life.

A postscript to the wedding was that Sheila's elder sister, Philippa, met my first cousin, John Scorer, at the occasion, and a year later got married also. Their children, Marcus and Sally, later became lifelong friends of their own cousins, our daughters Lindsay and Gemma. All in the family!

The first challenge that faced Sheila and me was to find a place to live. For both of us the character of our homes was immensely important. We had each suffered the trauma of being sent away from an intimate family environment to boarding school at a young age – in her case eight years old, in mine thirteen. We both worked at home for much of the time throughout our lives. We both valued the facilities of the city, but yearned for the peace of the countryside.

In my case, I had spent my teenage years at home in a wing of a remarkable Tudor pile, built by Henry VIII as one of his many hunting lodges, and which my parents had bought after my father moved up in the corporate world. This creaking old property, on the edge of the village of Oxted, was surrounded by four acres of largely wooded grounds, and boasted an Edwardian swimming pool (in which humans mingled with tadpoles during the summer months), a very uneven grass tennis court, and the largest cedar tree in England. We children adored it, and ever afterwards I have been addicted to the ambience of historical buildings.

Another incentive to buy a place was of course the imperative of getting onto the property ladder, as powerful then as it is today.

I had only a small sum in the bank, and being actors we had little hope at that time of raising a mortgage. However Sheila's father – a greatly respected farmer, both on his beloved land, and in the maelstrom of local and national agricultural politics – kindly lent us £3000 with which to try and find something. After much searching amongst the list of dismal London flats available within our modest price range, and in the areas we liked, we had almost given up hope when we came upon a place in a small nineteen twenties block close to Putney Heath. It was on the market for £4,250, which we could just afford. It was semi-basement, but had a sunny bow-windowed living room overlooking a patch of garden, a single bedroom, a decent sized kitchen and bathroom, and crucially a large, solid garage (probably alone worth around twenty times that amount today). We bought it, and joyfully set about decorating and altering it for our own needs – our first experience in property development.

However, we had lived there for less than three years before the onset of children forced us to rethink. We desperately needed more space, and as I had repaid Sheila's dad, and was by then earning reasonable money, we became bolder in our ambitions. After further numerous viewings of unaffordable three-bed apartments close to the obligatory green spaces, I came across a one-off opportunity.

Less than a mile from our Putney Heath flat stretched the broad spaces of Wimbledon Common. This is the most unique of London's marvellous parks, in that it is completely wild. Walking through it, one might imagine that one is in the New Forest, or even Exmoor. It is home to deer, foxes, badgers, hawks, and many other species of wild life, and within its many wooded acres one can ride horses, play golf, go winter skating, and pursue all manner of nature studies.

And at the edge of this space stands a small enclave of rather splendid period buildings, overlooking a grassy expanse towards the charming High Street of Wimbledon village. Chief amongst these is the magnificent Cannizaro House – built in the eighteenth century by the Italian Duke of Cannizarro (sic), friend and patron of William Pitt – but turned much later into a luxury hotel. A few doors along from this miniature palace stands a large white Regency mansion, divided into five spacious apartments, and known as The Keir. The whole top floor of this place then constituted a single flat, which was up for sale for the ridiculously low price of £11,000, the reason being it had only thirteen years remaining on its lease.

I went to view it, and immediately fell in love with its big rooms, its stunning views over the Common to the front, and the spreading lawns of the Cannizaro gardens at the rear, and with the evocative smell of old timber and stone that such antique buildings have.

I knew that the Government was planning new laws that would give security of tenure to lease holders, but even so this was a gamble. When I told my father about it, he said, "You're mad!"

But then he came to view it with me, and being equally addicted to historic dwellings, immediately exclaimed, "Buy it!"

So we did.

We were lucky in that we already had a buyer for our Putney Heath flat, in the shape of the glamorous actress, Cyd Hayman, whom I vividly remembered as being the first(?) to appear completely nude on television. I indelicately mentioned her bravery to her, but she laughed it off, quite unfazed.

We moved to Wimbledon, and made our usual improvements to the apartment's décor and layout, and there followed three years of grandiose domestic living, busy baby rearing, and various riotous show business parties, with (cheap) champagne filled baths, attended by famous and not so famous faces.

However, logistics intruded once again, and we were eventually forced to rethink. The flat was up three long flights of stairs, imposing, but exhausting. The business of carrying little Lindsay – with another one on the way – together with push chairs, shopping bags, et al, up and down, became simply too onerous. Furthermore, as two children grew more mobile, the need for our own garden would became imperative, despite having the wide spaces of the Common and the Cannizaro Gardens on our doorstep.

We began the search for a house.

As usual, our ambitions exceeded our means. All the fine Victorian and later-period houses that surrounded the Common were way beyond our budget. Those within it were in neighbourhoods too far from the parks and rural backdrops that we hankered for.

But finally I again came across something that presented a seriously daunting, but potentially major opportunity.

The summit of Richmond Hill offers a lively village street, access to the huge open spaces of Richmond Park, and magnificent views over the meadows and banks of the Thames river. John Mills, who I later directed in a musical of *Great Expectations,* lived in a grand house overlooking this famous view (he later sold it to Ronnie Wood of *The Rolling Stones,* who then passed it on to fellow Stone, Keith Richards. Signs of the times).

Descending from the village to the main township of Richmond itself – technically a separate Surrey town, but in fact, like Wimbledon, just another commuter suburb of West London – are several streets lined with commodious, semi-detached Victorian villas, mostly four stories high, including basement areas which were usually converted to self-contained flats. One of these monsters was for sale for a sum that was within our means. The reason being that it had been rented out for many years to what appeared to be a varying population of hippies, and was a complete mess.

The house boasted peeling wall-paper, rotting carpets, malfunctioning plumbing and electrics, graffiti on the walls, unspeakable detritus in every cupboard and corner, and a back yard that was more jungle than garden. However, the main structure was solid, the rooms were large and many, the jungle was quite big, and it was close to the summit of Richmond Hill. It had also been on the market for some months, and the owners were anxious to sell.

I spent many hours planning how to go about the restoration, and obtained various builders' estimates for the work. I reckoned that, with a now procurable mortgage, and a certain amount of design and work on my part, we could just about do it.

We sold our adored apartment at The Keir for more than twice what it had cost (this was the time of great property inflation), and rented a house in nearby Kew for six months, whilst we went about the renovation. With my fingers crossed, I hired an Irish builder who had come in with the lowest quote, and we began the immense task. He and his team knocked down walls, rewired and replumbed, installed imposing period fireplaces and wrought-iron verandas scavenged from the Chelsea reclamation yard, created extra bathrooms, put in new kitchens, redecorated the entire house, turned the basement into a cosy two-bed flat, and replanted the garden. We ended up with a rather splendid six bedroomed, three bathroomed house, with nursery and au pair accommodation, and enough income from the basement to cover the mortgage. It had been an exhausting, but highly instructive exercise. The total cost came in at £50,000, around one hundredth of its value today.

We lived there for seven years, until we moved to Bath and began another series of house hunting.

But that's a whole other tale.

CHAPTER EIGHT

Politics and Hamlet

The nineteen seventies and eighties was a time of huge political upheaval. The Wilson and Callaghan governments had resulted in a collapsing economy, a state virtually run by the unions, and a burgeoning class war between the haves and the have-nots. During the 1979 'Winter of Discontent', as some bright Shakespeare scholar had named it, the 'great' in Great Britain seemed to be dissolving for ever, and the land which we were taught had been such a force for (mostly) good, over almost two centuries of history, was sinking beneath the waves of the cold North Sea, never to emerge again as a major influence in the world. Humanity's proclivity for confrontation erupted. The unions were determined to demonstrate their power over the politicians, and all hell broke loose. Over the course of the coldest winter for decades, lorry drivers, dock workers, rubbish collectors, coal miners, hospital staff, ambulance drivers, grave diggers, printers, car makers – everyone it seemed with a grievance, however small, against anyone in authority, however nebulous, downed tools and joined the yelling picket lines in the biggest demonstration of attempted mass suicide the country had ever seen. Half the nation was put on part-time working, the army was called out to perform tasks it had never contemplated before, rubbish piled high in Trafalgar Square, bodies were left unburied in Liverpool and Manchester, the sick were denied access to hospitals, petrol stations closed for want of fuel, supermarkets closed for want of supplies, dead sheep were piled outside union offices by farmers with no feed for their stock, whole families shivered through winter's peak, without coal for their fires or food for their tables. It doesn't just happen in South American countries.

Margaret Thatcher came to power, much to the dismay of the Left and the relief of the Right. She set about trying to rectify matters, and over the course of three crucial victories finally pulled Britain back from the brink. The first was in the war with the unions, during which police battled with miners, led by the closet communist Arthur Scargill, and with the print unions, led by equally extremist shop stewards. The second was in the war with Argentina in the Falklands, which re-established Britain in the eyes of the world as a power to be reckoned with. And the third was over the economy, in which she freed banks, companies, entrepreneurs and working people, from the socialist stranglehold that had constricted them for so many years after the post-war boom. Labour supporters have still never forgiven her for her radical measures, though not the many thousands who, thanks to her, became home owners.

I was ever fascinated, inspired, and infuriated by the politics of the times. I am by nature inclined to the right of centre in my philosophy, believing that the enterprise of the individual always trumps that of big government. I haven't rigidly voted Conservative, preferring to judge a party by the quality of its policies and leader (Tony Blair for instance was the first Labour leader to make that party electable for almost twenty years – but then many would say he was not a true socialist).

The psychology of voters' leanings is a fascinating one, and I maintain that it has far more to do with the individual's mental makeup than with any intellectual analysis of systems.

My serious plays and novels invariably contain a political element. I quote here from a speech made by the central character in my novel, 'A Perfect Being':-

"Certainly our political affiliations are the result of instinct. Whether we are left or right leaning is determined by personality, not by logic or evidence. It depends how pessimistic or optimistic are our outlooks. How defensive or how bold. How cautious or how entrepreneurial.

The evidence of world history is quite clear on the subject of political systems. Liberal democracy, or private enterprise, or free capitalism, whatever you wish to call it, has proved beyond argument to be far and away the most successful of all the tried methods in the modern world. It has survived all the assaults from left and far right, from authoritarians and anarchists, from reactionaries and progressives. Those so-called developed nations which have adopted and promoted it from the original British creation, formulated by Adam Smith, John Locke, David Hume, etcetera, have succeeded – despite all the financial crises and crashes – far beyond any of their competitors. That much is self-evident. Its essence is the rights of the individual, not of the state.

Yet, despite that evidence, the left and the extreme right refuse to accept it. The compulsion to interfere with the free progression of such systems still infects much of the planet. Whether it is socialism, communism, despotism, or plain anarchy, the leaders of countries which do not have the liberal tradition constantly attempt to manipulate and subvert the natural evolution of societies, sometimes with the best of intentions, sometimes with the worst, but always to the effect of curtailing the freedom of their peoples, and leaving them worse off. Dictatorships exploit them, radical regimes oppress them, socialist movements attempt to command them. One could even claim that most wars originate because of them. Even in our own Western countries the left mistrusts what motivates and stimulates communities, and by insisting on authoritarian social changes, weakens their close-knit groups, traditions, and institutions. These in fact, initiated and driven by individuals, not by governments, have always been the engine which progresses civilisation. History proves it, but governments (and often voters) invariably forget it, and look to paternal authority to cure society's ills. Nothing impedes the human spirit except manipulation from above. And before the socialists protest, it is also the civic community which provides the best protection for the disadvantaged. The homeless, the destitute, look for help to local charities, churches, and authorities, rather than to big government – which, by constant tinkering with finances and social welfare, invariably distorts the natural order.

Of course the basic defences against misfortune are necessary – welfare benefits, healthcare, the rule of law – and these are all superior in the capitalist nations – but, by attempting to make them the government's monopoly and cure-all, the left's socialist reforms invariably backfire, and disrupt civil communities and economies rather than strengthen them. Bureaucracy and high taxation have ever been the enemy of economic progress."

A bit soap-boxy, but it describes my own beliefs, reinforced by the anguish of those desperate times.

The wisest comment on politics for me is this:- 'If you are not a socialist when you are young, you have no heart. If you are still a socialist when you are thirty, you have no brain.'

But that will get up the noses of a lot of lifelong lefties.

However, through all the turmoil, Sheila and I managed to keep our own ship afloat.

Before I met her, she had left the Guildhall with several awards, and had played seasons at Colchester and Bristol Old Vic, and the occasional part on television. During the early years of our marriage she played Richard Brier's fiancée, in a starry West End production of the Feydeau farce, *Cat Among The Pigeons*.

But she too had her setbacks. She was cast as the female lead in a John Mortimer play, which was then cancelled. She was approached to take over from Mia Farrow in a Broadway production, but was refused a Green Card by American Equity. She was offered a role in play starring Ralph Richardson and Peggy Ashcroft, but too late for our committed travel plans to be cancelled.

It is these kinds of disappointments that illustrate the dark side of the actor's profession. It is even harder for women in the business than for men. Firstly, there are fewer female roles in most scripts (although the modern era seems to be changing that, at least on TV). Secondly, an attractive leading lady all too often has a short career span. Few survive the onset of middle age, at least as headline figures. The list of beautiful girls who had the limelight early on and then faded away, is lengthy. It's not quite the same for men. An unfair fact of life.

Then, early on in our marriage, I had my one and only encounter with Laurence Olivier.

I had a good part in a delightful comedy titled *George and Margaret* by Gerald Savory, which starred Dora Bryan, a popular comedienne, and included in the cast a young Nigel Havers, with whom I was to become great friends.

Dora was an exuberant but scatty lady. One never quite knew where she would be on the stage, or what line she would come out with. However she could be very funny, and audiences loved her. She also knew almost everyone in show business.

Whilst on tour, she got an invitation for the whole cast to visit Cliff Richard for tea in his palatial Berkshire home, where he proved a charming host.

Then we went to Brighton, where Dora owned a hotel with her husband. A near neighbour at the time was Sir Laurence Olivier, who had moved to Brighton to escape the hurly-burly of London.

Olivier could claim to be the most famous actor of the twentieth century. His classical performances and productions, on stage and on film, had garnered more awards than one could count (he still holds the record, along with Spencer Tracey, for the number of male

Oscar nominations). He was the founder of the National Theatre, and the first actor ever elevated to the House of Lords.

Dora announced delightedly that the great man was going to come and see the midweek matinée, which threw the cast into a state of nervous anticipation. The performance went well, but afterwards I nipped off for some tea at a local café, assuming that Olivier might pop in to say hello to Dora, but little else. However, when I returned to the theatre, the stage doorman said, "Where have you been? Everyone's been looking for you. Laurence Olivier wants to meet you."

I raced along to Dora's dressing room, to find her sitting with Olivier, whilst his young son played on the floor beside them (what *he* thought of the show, I can't imagine). Olivier, in his sixties now, and rather frail looking, made some complimentary remark about my performance, but I was so flustered at meeting him that I barely took it in. Then, to hide my awkwardness, I turned my attention instead to his son, with some false avuncular comments. That is not the kind of response you show to such a great name, certainly not one as egotistical as Olivier. He was presumably looking for some theatrical interchange. He concluded the meeting fairly quickly, and departed.

"Missed your chance to join the National Theatre there, Robin," commented Dora. My ineptitude at the social graces had let me down again.

However by this time Nigel Havers and I had become very friendly, later holidaying together on Corfu with our respective wives. Nigel went on to make a name for himself in various film and TV roles, notably *Chariots of Fire* on the big screen, and *The*

Charmer on the small one. He became a client of the successful theatre agent, Michael Whitehall (father of comedian Jack Whitehall, star of numerous popular TV shows), who was a friend of ours, and who had coincidentally taken on Sheila as one of his very first protegées.

Late in 1974, Nigel was approached by some South African producers to play Hamlet the following year. Every summer the company mounted a Shakespeare production in their open-air theatre in Cape Town, and they would traditionally come to England to cast the major roles. Nigel was committed elsewhere, but suggested me instead. It was a part I had always said I would never dare attempt in Britain, as it would inevitably invite comparison with all the great Hamlets of the past. However South Africa was different, and Africa was a country I had always wanted to visit.

Also, by strange coincidence, I had just been asked to reprise a part I had played in London in *Not In The Book*, starring Wilfred Hyde White, well-known face of many British films, most notably as Colonel Pickering, Rex Harrison's confidant in *My Fair Lady*. This time the offer was for a South African tour of the production.

I met with the *Hamlet* producers – a formidable pair of ladies – and they offered me the role on the spot (with the partial incentive of knowing I might be in their country anyway). They then asked if I could suggest an actress to play Ophelia. I naturally suggested Sheila, and they were equally decisive in casting her.

The role in *Not In The Book* was not a big one, but as the dates miraculously fitted in with the *Hamlet* schedule, and the improvement to our budget would be considerable, I accepted it, even though it would mean my travelling out a month or two before Sheila.

By now our two daughters, Lindsay and Gemma, were aged three and six months. The logistics and the finances of the trip were going to be a considerable challenge. We would have to cover the cost of the children's air fares, and also work out how they would be cared for during rehearsals, and the several weeks run of the play. We solved the first problem by renting out our new home in Richmond, and the second by bringing with us as nanny, Sheila's younger cousin, Marylin, who jumped at the chance of coming to Africa.

The year we spent in that remarkable country was memorable for a host of reasons. The tour I did with Wilfred Hyde White, produced by South Africa's major impresario, Pieter Toerien, was a kaleidoscope of performances in the big cities, invitations to wealthy theatre-goers' houses, and explorations of the vast interior of the country. Wilfred himself was a genial old British gentleman, who was in serious debt to the Hollywood tax collectors, but nevertheless insisted on treating the cast to lavish lunches at all the best restaurants. The company were fun, and it was a joyous experience.

Then came *Hamlet.*

The problem of our living arrangements in Cape Town was hugely aided by another happy coincidence – the fact that an uncle of Sheila's from Wales lived there, was a successful and well-connected businessman, and was thrilled at having his niece and family come visiting the country. He arranged for us to rent the home of the Dutch Ambassador in Weinstein, an affluent Cape Town suburb.

This lovely house came with sunny, bougainvillea-draped terraces, an acre of flower-bedecked gardens, splendid swimming pool, and various attached black gardeners and house-maids. We could never have afforded it on our salaries, but Uncle Jimmy generously offered to pay half the rent. Where the Ambassador and his family were, we never discovered.

Sheila made the daunting journey out from England on her own with the children. How she managed the trip, together with luggage, push chairs, one energetic three year-old, and one sick baby – enduring almost missed flights, non-functioning airport escalators, a dearth of clean nappies, and uncaring French hostesses, I will never know. But she got there, exhausted but triumphant, and we moved into our splendid new home.

The open-air theatre at Maynardville is an enchanting venue similar to the one at Regents Park – but with better weather – and producing similar productions. The producers had also hired from the UK the deep-voiced Shakespearian actor, Joseph O'Conor, to play Claudius, which he had already played at Stratford. Cecilia Sonnenberg, wealthy South African society lady, and a director of the theatre, was to play Gertrude, and a number of local actors from around the country played all the other roles.

It was the first year that apartheid was relaxed, and blacks were allowed into the theatres and cinemas – not that many could afford to. Theatre people all over the country, who had long campaigned for the result, were celebrating the fact.

We rehearsed for a month, during which there were many enjoyable social events in that benign climate – parties around our swimming pool, barbecues in various lovely gardens, weekend trips up Table Mountain, or to the surrounding beaches and countryside.

I came to rehearsals already having learned most of Hamlet's lines (it's the longest part in Shakespeare with nearly 1500 of them), and I immersed myself in the role. It came much more easily than the various, rather insipid Shakespearian young man's parts that I had played previously, and which I could never quite get to grips with. This was a multi-faceted character, with dramatically defined changes of mood, and superbly constructed speeches. The director, Leslie French, and I initially got on well, and he was a great help with the part, treating the whole play in a traditional, un-tricksy way. Sheila also identified well with Ophelia, although three year-old Lindsay was traumatised by watching her mother go mad, reportedly die, and then be buried in a realistic grave dug into the ground.

Then came a rather unhappy crisis towards the end of rehearsals. Leslie wished to repeat a device for the curtain call which he had created for an earlier production. He wanted to avoid the traditional cast line-up across the stage, and instead simply show each of the half-dozen main characters standing on various outcrops of the tiered set, and illuminated one by one out of the darkness by spotlights. This was very effective visually.

However, when I asked how the rest of the cast would then be given their curtain call, he said, "Oh, they won't. There's no need for the minor characters to take a bow."

I felt this was greatly unfair on the large majority of the cast, who all had their friends and families coming to the show. There followed some argument between myself, Leslie, and the directors of the theatre. We could not reach an agreement, and eventually, in my usual undiplomatic manner, I said that I would not come on for the call unless everyone else did also.

I was of course in an impregnable position over the matter, and Leslie was forced to resort to a traditional line-up. However it caused a lot of bad feeling, and soured the final days of rehearsal. I was only a little consoled when some members of the cast came and thanked me afterwards for standing up for them.

We opened to what I must admit were mixed notices. I received one rave, in the national Afrikaans paper, and one or two ambivalent ones in the English papers. Sheila's Ophelia was generally well praised. Our performances improved further as the weeks went by. I've often thought it's a pity that critics have to come to first nights.

We stayed in South Africa for further months, travelling up to Johannesburg, where I played Ferdinand in *The Tempest* (another dull juvenile part), holidaying in the Drakensberg Mountains, and going on safari in the huge Kruger game park. The time was only marred by the discovery of baby Gemma sitting out in the sunlight, on a lawn a hundred miles from the nearest doctor or hospital, with a mouthful of what might have been poisonous mushrooms. I had to force feed her with a potion of salt and mustard to make her vomit, the effect of which almost choked her to death anyway. She repeated the trick a week later, but this time there was a hospital and stomach pumps within reach.

The whole experience was a memorable one, and we seriously considered staying in South Africa, even though the politics were still problematic, and the show business industry limited.

However, we were forced to reconsider because of another urgent problem on the home property front.

CHAPTER NINE

Villains and Heroes

We had let the Richmond house whilst we were away, for a sizeable sum, to what seemed an eminently respectable family. The husband claimed to be a retired high-ranking officer in the Royal Navy, he was married to an attractive blonde Swedish wife, and they had a sweet young daughter. For the first couple of months that we spent in South Africa, the rents arrived safely at my bank. Then they dried up.

There was little we could do about it from that distance. After various unanswered letters and phone calls, we eventually put my family solicitor onto it. He set legal balls rolling, but warned us that the tenancy laws might make it a long process.

Worse was to come. When we eventually arrived back in the UK, now seriously in debt because of the lost rents, the family refused to leave the house, slamming the door in my face and daring us to do our worst. Poor Sheila had to take the children and retreat to her parents' home on the farm in Wales (much to the delight of the girls), whilst I stayed behind in London to try and rectify the situation. There followed several weeks of abortive threats, legal summonses, and aggressive confrontations. Finally, the family simply disappeared overnight, still owing us several thousand pounds.

But then I achieved the most satisfying piece of poetic justice anyone could wish for.

Once back in our home, we discovered that the fraudsters had been living the high life at other people's expense. The kitchen drawers were full of champagne corks, the nanny's room was full of dirty sheets, the local shops were all owed large sums in outstanding bills. I also learned that the 'Commander' had been building a substantial house for his family in nearby Sheen, but that work had halted on this because the builders had also not been paid. It appeared that the man made his living by doing dubious export and import deals with Russia, and that, once the money ran out from the last one, he was bereft of other sources until the next one came along.

His mistake was in not giving a forwarding address for his mail – for obvious reasons. I was therefore able to open (illegally) the deluge of writs and begging letters that came through the door. I discovered that the family had put a large stock of furniture and other belongings into the Harrods Storage Depository, whilst awaiting completion of their new house. Furthermore, that he had not been paying the rental charges, along with all the other bills.

Harrods began sending letters threatening to put the possessions to auction if the bill wasn't paid within a certain time limit. I conferred with my solicitor as to whether we could make use of the situation. He said, yes, we certainly could, provided we kept quiet as to how we had come about the knowledge.

I had by now discovered where the family were living – in

another large house, presumably also rent free. I did not of course inform them of the Harrods threat, nor did I forward on any of their incoming mail, and my solicitor put in a second claim on the stock. The deadline came and went, and the effects were duly auctioned off. They evidently included some quite valuable furniture and paintings, because the sum realised was enough to pay the Harrods bill, all our back rent, all our costs and legal fees, and also most of the local traders, whom I had alerted to the situation.

I wish I could have seen the swindler's face when he discovered what had happened. I was tempted to write a play about the episode, but never did. Truth is stranger than fiction.

I was now back to acting, writing, and some directing in the UK. I had already directed a couple of my own plays on tour and in rep, and also a musical Christmas show at the Phoenix Theatre in London, *The Magic of Houdini,* which featured spectacular magic effects imported at considerable cost from the USA – amongst them the obligatory disappearing caged lion (in our case a St Bernard dog for safety reasons), and a bewildering illusion where the scantily clothed heroine was supported lying on the points of three large sabres, two of which were then whisked away by the magician.

Then, shortly after our return from South Africa, I was commissioned to direct, or rather redirect, a musical version of Charles Dickens's *Great Expectations*, starring John Mills as Pip's adopted uncle, Joe Gargery. The show was in trouble, partly because it was overbalanced by the need to make Mills's part larger than it was in the book, in order to justify his presence. Sir John, as he was shortly to become, was a delight to work with, and was still an able song-and-dance performer from his early days in review. I tried to manipulate the scenes and cut extraneous stuff, but there was little I could do, and it never got to London.

I was also contracted to direct and act in a comedy titled *My Fat Friend,* produced by Derek Nimmo in Hong Kong of all places. Derek was a well known comedy actor, parodying upper class English idiots. He was far from an idiot himself, establishing a brilliant business mounting shows with starry TV faces at luxury hotels all over the Middle and Far East. He played his old Etonian persona to the hilt, and was known by every manager and *maitre d'hotel* across Asia as 'Mr Nimmo'.

I and the cast, which included Paula Wilcox from TV's *Man About The House,* and Ian Lavender from *Dad's Army,* had an enjoyable couple of weeks sampling the luxuries of Hong Kong's Shangri La Hotel. It was my first experience of the Far East, although much later Sheila and I made memorable stopovers in Singapore, Hong Kong, Bangkok, and the Arab states, during our annual flights to Australia (more later).

Next came the commission to direct *Suez* by the prolific writer Royce Ryton, and starring my old accomplice, Roy Dotrice, as Sir Anthony Eden, Prime Minster at the time of the epoch-changing Suez crisis.

Royce was a hugely camp, hugely flamboyant, and hugely eccentric actor/writer who had had a big success with the aforementioned *Crown Matrimonial,* and several near misses since. He was like a fictional character, forever parodying Oscar Wilde with his exotic clothes, billowing hair, and exaggerated vocal delivery. He was obsessed with royalty, history, and gay scenarios (although married to the sister of politician and author, Ludovic Kennedy). He wrote his plays with a quill pen, and had a deafening laugh and a ferocious temper.

I encountered that temper from time to time, when forced to demand some cuts in the play, which was running at three hours long, but the crises were always forgotten in the shadow of the next one. We remained amicable associates until much later, when I was running the Theatre Royal Bath, when I tried to promote a couple of his ingenious later pieces, without success.

Suez was not a great play, but we had a modestly successful tour, followed by a brief run at the Savoy Theatre. Roy Dotrice later went off to spend the rest of his career in America.

I was then asked by the same producer, Michael Cooper, to direct the ambitious musical, *Dean,* based on the tragic life of the young film star, James Dean. The character list included, not only the actor himself, but also Clark Gable, Natalie Wood, Elizabeth Taylor, and various of the Hollywood moguls involved with Dean's all too brief career. Consequently, finding the right actors who could also sing the challenging numbers, posed an immense task. We held many auditions, and eventually found a cast which I was enthusiastic about. All except for the central character. He not only had to sing, but also had to convincingly portray the tormented energy of the Hollywood icon, who had died in a car crash after making only three films.

The main backer of the show was a twenty year-old member of the vast Thyssen dynasty, founders of much of Germany's industrial might. This inexperienced youth fancied himself as an impresario. He now fired the producer, took over the reins himself, and decided the right actor would only be found in America. He consequently flew there with a boyfriend, leaving me to continue the search in London. After many more attempts, I discovered an exciting talent in the shape of the actor, Glenn Conway, who could not only play the guitar and sing, but had the right intensity for the role.

However, at the same time Master Thyssen in America decided that he had also found his James Dean, and, without consulting me, announced it to the press, who were all by now agog with the story of the hunt. This actor arrived at Heathrow, to be met by a bevy of reporters and camera men, and the story made all the front pages.

I then met him for the first time. I found a pretty young lad, with blue eyes and a charming smile, but little of the experience or inner angst that the role required. I had to fire him on the spot.

By now time was getting short. No tour was planned, and the show was due to open for previews directly in London, in only three weeks' time – an impossible rehearsal period for such a large scale musical. I insisted that Glenn Conway should play the part, and also that the first preview date should be delayed for a week. In the following confrontation with the young producer over this, I tried to explain to him the huge risks of opening an under-rehearsed musical cold in London, but he wouldn't listen. He insisted on his actor, and his timescale. He had been brought up to believe that money could solve anything.

I went home disconsolate, and the next morning was woken by a phone call from a reporter on a national newspaper, asking if I had any comment on the news that I had been sacked from the show. I was of course at a loss for a reply. My contract had been broken in a myriad different ways, but it wasn't worth going to war over it.

I then learned that a director from America had been flown in, who promptly fired the American actor, reinstated Glenn Conway, and attempted to mount the piece within the three weeks timescale. Somehow he managed to get it on, but in a much simplified form, with an incomplete set and effects. It received fairly scathing notices, and lasted only a month.

There's no business like show business.

CHAPTER TEN

Caveman to James Bond

I am again getting ahead of myself.

Some time before the *Dean* episode I had tasted film stardom.

Early in my career I had played a featured role in a film written and directed by Val Guest, called *The Day The Earth Caught Fire.* It was prophetic in that it depicted a planet growing increasingly hotter (in that instance nudged towards the sun by atomic bomb tests). In the movie I experienced my first death scene – victim of a typhoid epidemic brought on by the catastrophe.

Val Guest, an amiable man with a reputation for seducing all his leading ladies (so what's new?), had now been commissioned by Hammer Films to write and direct a sequel to the highly successful *One Million Years BC*, the picture that had made Raquel Welch an international star. This one was titled *When Dinosaurs Ruled The Earth*, and was to star another voluptuous American actress, Victoria Vetri – a former *Playboy's* 'Playmate of the Year'.

The male lead was to be cast in the UK, and my agent sent me up for it.

I met Val, and we reminisced about *The Day The Earth Caught Fire* (in my opinion his best film), but then he said he thought I was too young-looking to play the hunky caveman in the wildly anachronistic *Dinosaurs.*

I pondered on this. I was working at the time on a TV show at the BBC, and I asked my makeup man there if he could knock me up a beard and moustache, which he obligingly did. I then rang Val up at his home in St Johns Wood, and asked to meet him again. I did so wearing all the extra hair, which made me look considerably older. Val laughed, and said, "All right, I'll give you a film test."

One other actor was tested. That was Hal Hamilton, who I knew well, as he had been in my class at RADA. Hal was American, handsome, and did body-building, so I assumed he would get the part. However, to my surprise, the producers gave it to me, provided I put on a stone in weight (I am six feet tall, but have never weighed more than 75kg).

They sent me to see a doctor, who put me on a regime of pills, telling me that they would make me hungry, that I should eat as much as possible, and that I should be sure to convert the extra weight into muscle, not fat. He advised me to get a Bullworker, the muscle-building gadget much advertised by the ex-Mr Universe, Charles Atlas.

The pills were of course anabolic steroids, but they didn't have the invidious reputation that they have today. I began swallowing them, pigging on big meals, and working on my Bullworker, and within a week or two was showing muscles I'd never had before.

We filmed *Dinosaurs* mostly on location in the Canary Isles. I spent most of my time racing up and down mountains, saving Victoria Vetri from horrible fates, and spear-fighting empty spaces which were later to be filled with animated monsters. I did all my own stunts, some mildly hazardous, some distinctly uncomfortable, as when being hoisted into the air by a monstrous pterodactyl claw attached to a harness hidden under my loin cloth.

The chief attribute of steroids is that they make you feel invincible (a large part of their value for athletes). What with a very early morning start for makeup and travel to location, and late nights living it up in the hotel disco with the company, I existed on four to five hours sleep a night for several months. I have never felt better.

The other result of taking the pills was that I continued to put on weight and muscle throughout the filming. However, as many of the scenes were shot out of sequence because of the logistics, it often appeared in the final cut that the ordeals I had suffered were actually making me lose weight!

The dialogue, such as it was, consisted of a lot of bizarre grunts and shouts as part of a wholly fictitious language invented by Val Guest for the screenplay. His theory was that audiences would gradually become familiar with the words through repetition. I don't think they ever did, but it scarcely seemed to matter since subtlety of plot was never a feature of such epics.

Victoria Vetri was a sweet but rather dizzy creature, under contract to Columbia, and addicted to a multi-coloured collection of pills in true Hollywood tradition. She never quite knew what her eccentric lines were, or in which direction she was supposed to be running, but she was photogenic, and I suspect came out of the picture somewhat better than my bearded and stone-age faced caveman did. She moved on to a rather unhappy life, which included an unfulfilled Columbia contract, and a prison sentence for attempted murder of her abusive husband.

The film was found mildly laughable by the critics, but was spectacular, and was actually nominated for an Oscar for its special effects (the Oscars showed a clip of me fighting a Tyrannosaurus Rex – Tarzan never did that!). These were created by Jim Danforth, pupil of the great Ray Harryhausen who had invented the technique, and it was the last of such to use his laborious method of minutely manipulating plasticine models, before the advent of CGI made things so much easier. Nowadays the majority of historical backgrounds and dramatic effects are created digitally.

Shortly after *Dinosaurs* ended, I was given the central role in a hilariously misconceived James Bond spoof titled *Zeta One ('The Love Factor'* in the USA). My character was called James Word, and I had to introduce myself as, "Word. James Word. My word is my bond," which the writer evidently thought extremely witty.

I had to weave my way through an impossibly convoluted story, which involved villains James Robinson Justice and Charles Hawtrey kidnapping half-clothed girls and sending them to be brainwashed by the queen of another planet, played by Dawn Addams (don't ask). There were the obligatory fights, car chases, and bedroom scenes, and the girls got progressively more naked as the story unfolded.

Once filming was done I assumed that would be the last of it, but then some time later, I was called back for another week's filming, in which I had to explain the incomprehensible plot to bewildered viewers, whilst playing strip poker with a beautiful Scandinavian actress named Yutte Stensgaard. Naturally she lost the poker game, whilst I earned more money. I in fact made more on that low-budget piece than I had done on *Dinosaurs.*

The filming was enlivened for me by the fact that my real love interest in it was played by Anna Gael, star of various continental films. We had one long bedroom scene together, during which I had to seductively pull both a nude Anna, and a large double bed, towards me, using the cord of a telephone resting in her hands. The laws of physics of course made this impossible, so the director had two hefty stage hands crouch down behind the bed, pushing as I pulled. We rehearsed the scene with Anna in her dressing gown, then the director said, "All right, everyone, let's go for a take. Anna, can we lose the gown, please."

At which she replied, "Oh, but now these two boys will be looking straight up my bottom!"

There was a slight hiatus, during which the director moved the men sideways, and commanded them to keep their heads down as they pushed, and the men replied, "Don't worry, luv, we promise we won't look."

I was watching from the other side of the bed, and to their credit they kept their promise.

Then, whilst Anna and I lay together beneath the sheets, passing the time during the interminable lighting process, we chatted. She told me that she had been proposed to by Viscount Weymouth, heir to the huge Longleat estate near Bath, whom she had known whilst they were art students together in Paris. He was a wildly eccentric figure, following in the footsteps of his equally eccentric father, the Marquess of Bath. The son delighted in painting lewd murals around the cellars of the stately home, and reportedly kept a number of 'wifelets' in cottages on the estate.

I asked Anna whether she loved him, and she replied, "Oh no, but he's a good friend, and all I have to do would be to give him a male heir in exchange for becoming the Marchioness. Then we would both be free to conduct our separate love lives."

This she subsequently did. Whether it brought her happiness, history doesn't recall. She still lives in splendour at Longleat as I write. After our move to Bath, I would often take the children to visit the Longleat Safari Park, and was always tempted to drop in and say hello again, but never did. Hard to say, "Your Grace" to someone you have spent several hours in bed with.

A postscript to my brief career as a film star was that, shortly after the premiere of *Dinosaurs* (a full red carpet affair at the Empire, Leicester Square), Sheila and I were invited by the publicity department to come to Judy Garland's fifth wedding reception. We had no connection whatsoever with Garland, but I think they needed to make up the numbers.

She was in London at the time, making a last-gasp concert appearance at the Talk Of The Town, both her finances and her health being in very poor state. The wedding reception was held at the famous Quaglino's restaurant in Jermyn Street. When we arrived at the appointed hour, we found the big room cleared, a band playing at one end, and a bevy of reporters and camera men waiting for the star's arrival. They outnumbered the guests by two to one. We gleaned from the publicity man that Garland was marrying a much younger night-club owner named Mickey Deans, and that the wedding was largely a publicity stunt to publicise the launching of a chain of 'Judy Garland' cinemas (since disappeared).

We were given a glass of champagne, and awaited the entrance of the happy couple. They finally arrived an hour late, and the band struck up 'Somewhere Over The Rainbow'. It was a sad sight. Judy was only forty seven, but looked seventy seven. She tottered in, a tiny figure on matchstick-thin legs, supported by the muscular figure of her new husband, and accompanied by singer Johnny Ray, the best man, in white tuxedo. During the applause and the flashing of camera bulbs, I whispered to Sheila, "She looks as though she won't last six months."

In fact she lasted less than that. She was found dead of an overdose in her rented Belgravia cottage three months later, after years of trying to combat the pressures of show business adulation through drugs and alcohol. A tragic end to a unique Hollywood figure.

I have always loved the cinema above all other forms of entertainment. I was an avid cinema goer ever since my mother first took me to see *Bambi* – the shooting of whose own mother traumatised generations of children – followed by *Mighty Joe Young* (the precursor to *King Kong)*, which was equally traumatic.

As a young child I was convinced that the roaring lion, announcing the start of every MGM movie, had to be a real beast precariously chained behind the screen.

During the classic days of Hollywood in the nineteen fifties, sixties, and seventies, I must have seen hundreds of films – enthralled by the Westerns, thrilled by the musicals, engrossed by the Hitchcocks, fascinated by the continental pictures, inspired by the political and domestic dramas. I would never miss any film starring Brando, James Stewart, Cary Grant, Gregory Peck, Henry Fonda, Jack Lemmon – or later, Al Pacino, Daniel Day Lewis, Tom Hanks, Tommy Lee Jones, Denzel Washington, Gene Hackman, Matthew McConaughey, etc, etc.

I have often debated with fellow addicts, who has been the greatest male star of all time. Opinions and audience surveys have differed greatly. However, for me – assuming stardom is a compilation of acting talent, sex appeal, list of distinguished credits, and longevity – then the answer has to be Paul Newman.

And the women, ah, the women! There are few female stars who would for me make a picture imperative to see (except for Audrey Hepburn), but there are equally few who I haven't lusted after in my fantasies. I have also often discussed the mystery of female beauty. No one has been able to explain to me the scientific criteria by which good looks are determined. If one takes from that era at random, Grace Kelly, Sophia Loren, Brigitte Bardot, and Audrey Hepburn – they were all universally acclaimed models of female beauty, yet all so varied in their looks as to be almost different species. So what is the mysterious factor? Nature moves in strange ways.

My own cinematic career ended with two attempts at creating iconic British heroes – as a writer, Horatio Nelson, and as an actor, the real James Bond. The two occasions, separated by only a few months, were oddly linked.

CHAPTER ELEVEN

More Heroes

In 1971, when we were still living at The Keir, and our firstborn, Lindsay, was only six months old, I was given the dream job of writing the screenplay for an epic movie about the Battle of Trafalgar. This was probably the greatest sea battle ever fought, and certainly the one with the most radical effect on the balance of world power, ending as it did Napoleon's hopes of dominating the oceans, and leading to his eventual defeat at Waterloo, thus establishing Britain as the world's foremost power.

The commission came from the producers of the James Bond films, Harry Salzman and Albert 'Cubby' Broccoli, who had recently had a big success with their Second World War film *The Battle Of Britain*, and were looking for another large-scale battle film to produce. They had apparently hired other established screen writers for the job, but were unimpressed by the results and were looking for a new talent to bring freshness to the idea.

My unhappy experience over *The Hero* was a recent event, but on the strength of it my clever agent, Richard Stone, sent the text to the *Trafalgar* tycoons, and then arranged for me to meet their executive producer, Benny Fisch. He told me that the company wanted a draft screenplay in ten weeks time to fit in with their pre-production schedule – did I think I could do it? With fingers crossed I said yes. He then asked how much a week I needed to live on. I didn't think fast enough, and said £100, which was roughly the truth. He said, okay, we'll pay you a thousand pounds for the ten weeks' work.

If I had doubled my quote I'm sure he would have agreed.

However, I then embarked on one of the most fascinating tasks of my career.

It was springtime and, inspired by Sheila's and my own joint love of the countryside, I suggested that we let the newly acquired Wimbledon flat and rent somewhere for the ten weeks, away from London in the romantic West Country. After a couple of days frantically searching through Devon and Cornwall, and finding nothing that matched our rural dream, I then followed a trail of enquiries at various village shops and post offices, which led to an enchanting cottage in the tiny Dorset hamlet of Long Bredy. The gracious couple who owned it were heading to France for the summer, and letting their three bedroomed period house, together with its classic English garden and kitchen garden, small swimming pool, and housekeeper, Mags, for the princely sum of £40 a week. They hoped it wasn't too much for us. I didn't tell them that we were letting our London flat for twice that.

Sheila, I, and baby Lindsay, moved down to this idyllic house, with its views over the sheep-dotted Dorset hills, its garden full of roses, asparagus beds, and raspberry bushes, and the motherly Mags, who lived in the village and who turned out to be a wonderful cook, as well as knowing all the gossip for miles around. Mags also acted as baby sitter for Lindsay when we wanted time off to explore the nearby villages and stately homes, and the seaside town of Weymouth with its fishing fleet and seafood bistros. Thomas Hardy's ghost lingered everywhere.

I had brought with me a car-boot full of books about Nelson and Trafalgar, and I steeped myself in the subject.

Admiral Viscount Horatio Nelson was of course England's greatest ever naval hero. He had established a towering reputation in British folklore through his victories at Cape St Vincent, The Nile, and Copenhagen, through his habit of disobeying orders and using unorthodox battle tactics, through his brilliant attention to the welfare and training of the sailors under his command, and last but not least through his notorious romance with Lady Emma Hamilton. The fact that he himself was killed during the final stages of the tremendous Trafalgar encounter cemented his historic reputation for ever. It is not surprising that his column in Trafalgar Square is the highest memorial in the land.

Also, as I said in my introduction to the finished screenplay, 'The sight of a two hundred feet high, three-decker man-of-war under full sail with all guns blazing must have been one of the most magnificent ever created by human design.'

I finished the work just within the ten weeks, working night and day, and we regretfully left Mags and our rural idyll, and returned to London. There followed several weeks of waiting whilst the producers assessed the screenplay and its filmic implications. I never in fact met with the two company heads, Saltzman and Broccoli, as all my dealings were with Benny Fisch. However, everyone seemed happy with the script, apart from wanting me to turn Emma Hamilton into an orgy seeking trollop, which was quite inaccurate, and which I fought strongly against.

The main worry, however, was how to stage the battle itself. I had devised the script so that no more than two full-sized ships would be in view at any one time. But the panoramic scenes of the encounter were to be filmed using over a hundred model vessels floating on the waters of a huge 'tank' at Malta, which was complete with wind and wave making features, and often used by film companies for sea scenes. Such a feat, directing motorised models (this was before the days of digitalisation), had never been attempted before, and the feeling grew that it might be impracticable. Also the estimated costs of filming such an epic were rising alarmingly.

In the end the producers abandoned the idea. My paltry thousand pounds was no doubt offset against the profits from their next Bond picture.

It was of course another big disappointment. And it was compounded many years later, when the BBC took up the script again, when searching for a vehicle to celebrate the 2005 bicentenary of the battle. We almost got to the point of contract on it, when the accountants stepped in and again proclaimed that it would be too expensive, even though most of the costs would be covered by joint American and British film companies. The Beeb instead resorted to the traditional method of having learned historians waffling in front of famous paintings – much cheaper than using real ships and guns.

Trafalgar is a fabulous subject for a movie. It has politics, personal drama, romance, suspense, and breath-taking spectacle. One day someone will make it.

Then, shortly after, I was to meet Harry Saltzman and 'Cubby' Broccoli for real.

Sean Connery had established James Bond as a hero like no other, and began a franchise that looks to continue for ever. He was followed briefly by a statuesque model with little acting experience called George Lazenby. After this man's single uninspiring Bond movie, the producers announced that they would start looking for someone else for the next one, *Live And Let Die*.

All the leading young actors in London were put up by their agents for the part, including myself. The initial filtering-out interviews were conducted by a production assistant called Dyson Lovell, whom I knew because he had been a year ahead of me at RADA. Dyson had the body of a Mr Universe, and could have been a candidate for Bond himself, except that had given up acting for producing, and was gay.

When we met at the smart Mayfair offices of the company, Dyson said, "Well, Robin, I'll get you to meet Harry and Cubby, and I'll give you some tips. First of all dress conservatively, in a business suit with white shirt and not too flashy tie. Make yourself look as hunky as possible – put shoulder pads in your jacket and lifts in your shoes. Be sure to get into the conversation that you like girls, because they are fearful of casting someone gay as James Bond. And last but not least, practise your walk. They will decide from the way you walk into their big office, and all the way from the door to their desk, whether you are James Bond material or not."

When the day came, I put on my only tailored suit, added the home-made shoulder pads and shoe lifts, and returned to the offices. In the outer waiting room were a number of other hopefuls, most of whom I knew at least vaguely, all dressed in smart suits, probably with shoulder pads and shoe lifts.

"Hi, Robin. Hi, Simon. Hi, Ian," we greeted each other in deep voices, and with Bondian expressions.

One by one the others were called through a big mahogany door into the main office. When my turn came I went, quaking inwardly, through the door, and did my James Bond walk (with difficulty as the carpet pile was several inches deep) towards the big desk at the far end of the room. Behind it sat the two stout Hollywood moguls, one actually smoking a cigar if memory serves.

The interview passed in a haze – the standard listing of my career credits, with the obligatory mention that I had had various romantic female encounters, and was now married. The pair were mildly surprised when they discovered that I was the same Robin Hawdon who had written their *Trafalgar* screenplay, and they knew about my previous starring roles, but thankfully hadn't actually seen the films.

Then, midway through the ordeal, one of them turned to the other and said, "I think we should test this boy, Harry. Whaddaya think?"

The other nodded, and said to me, "Yeh, yeh. We'll give you a film test, kid. Coupl'a weeks. We'll let your agent know."

I thanked them, did my James Bond walk back to the door, then rushed off to the nearest telephone to tell my agent.

The two weeks passed, with both Sheila and I on tenterhooks. Then my agent rang to say, "Sorry, Robin, but the test has been cancelled by the film's director, Guy Hamilton. They didn't give a reason."

I was naturally shattered, but remembering my experience with Val Guest and the test for *Dinosaurs,* I decided not to let the matter rest. I somehow managed to get an interview with Guy Hamilton, I forget where. I donned my Bond outfit and went to see him. He was an austere looking man, who was polite, but strangely uncommunicative about the reasons for cancelling the test. I left none the wiser.

However, a week or so later, I opened my morning paper to see the headline, 'Roger Moore to be the next James Bond.'

Moore was already well-known as 'Ivanhoe' and 'The Saint' on TV, and through various starring film parts. He had been in the frame for Bond for a while, but previous commitments and Sean Connery's monopoly of the role had prevented it. He was considerably older and heavier than me, and the negotiations had probably been going on all through the audition process.

In retrospect it was a lucky escape. I would never have lived up to Sean Connery's iconic portrayal, my marriage would probably never have survived the Hollywood holocaust, and I would not have had the happy and fulfilled writer's life that followed.

However, my acting career was not quite done with yet. A year or two later, after yet more tours and rep parts, I won a leading role in a half-hour ITV play titled *Spasms* (they made such things in those days). This was a very funny script by Alex Shearer, about two disparate husbands waiting nervously in the waiting room of a hospital maternity ward, whilst their respective wives were giving birth next door. Playing the other husband was the up-and-coming actor, Jonathan Pryce.

Jonathan and I got on well, and we had fun making the show. It received very complimentary reviews, but then we went off and thought no more about it. However, some months later, the producer, Michael Mills, rang me up and said, "Robin, ITV liked the show so much they want to make a comedy series out of it. They have commissioned Alex Shearer to write six episodes based on the two characters. They want you and Jonathan to repeat your performances."

This was good news. There had been various two-handed TV series, such as *Steptoe and Son, The Likely Lads, The Liver Birds,* etc, but I had never starred in such a vehicle.

Then the story took another turn. Michael rang me again, and said, "Jonathan Pryce doesn't want to do it. He has his eyes set on bigger things." (He in fact went on to play *Hamlet* at the Royal Court shortly after, and thence to film stardom). "However, what do you think of the idea of Michael Crawford?"

Michael was already a hugely popular TV star after his inspired idiot portrayal of Frank Spencer in *Some Mothers Do 'Ave 'Em.*

"Would he do it?" I asked.

Michael Mills replied, "Well, since I directed *Some Mothers*, and I know he's looking for something different, I think I might be able to persuade him."

This he did. I met Michael Crawford for the first time, and found a very friendly, very funny, and hyperactive thespian, brimming with ideas for the show and for his character. He had by now starred in various plays and musicals in London, and was as big a name in the theatre as on TV.

The theme of our show was that of two incompatible men,

and their wives and new-born babies, who, after the first episode (a repeat of the maternity ward play), then found themselves neighbours in a genteel middle-class London street. Michael played an uncouth bearded Cockney, who had turned his home into an unkempt slum, in contrast to my pristine domestic abode. The scripts were funny, and Michael certainly had his wish to be seen as something different to Frank Spencer.

Michael and I got on fine, which was just as well since he could be very intolerant of people he didn't consider up to the job. He was the archetypal actor – obsessed with his current role, extremely egotistical, but at the same time very lively and entertaining when in company.

The early reviews were again propitious, if a little taken aback at his new persona. The viewing figures were respectable, if not record breaking, but Michael Mills told me that it was likely they would take off with the second series, which was usually what happened after audiences had grown familiar with the characters, and the nostalgia factor had been added. Things looked good.

Then, some six months after we had completed the first series, and when the writer was well into the scripts for the next, Michael Crawford announced that he was breaking contract, as he'd been offered the title role in the musical *Barnum*. He later claimed that it was because audiences hadn't taken to his character in *Chalk And Cheese*, but I suspect that was only part of the story.

I was back to square one again.

CHAPTER TWELVE

Life Change

The disappointment over *Chalk and Cheese* compounded a feeling that had been growing in me for some time. Acting may be a glamorous profession in the public's eyes, but in reality it can be a highly unsettling, insecure, and mentally destructive business. Of course it is fun when flying off to some spectacular location, or exploring rural Britain whilst on tour, or when enjoying the delights of London's night life while in a successful show on Shaftesbury Avenue. And the camaraderie within companies is usually extremely close and entertaining (not to say romantic), if ephemeral. However, in between such highlights, it is often a frustrating and unsettling existence of waiting for the telephone to ring, worrying about one's seesawing finances, and dithering over whether to accept a mediocre part in a second-rate rep production. Or even whether to plan a holiday. Sheila and I several times had to abandon a seaside holiday in mid-term in order to come back for an audition, which then didn't land us the part. One's life is never completely one's own.

And even the process of acting itself is not really a healthy one. Yes, it is fascinating when delving into the personality and mannerisms of a well conceived character, and interpreting the subtleties of a brilliantly written play (but how often do those come along?). The rehearsal period can be an absorbing time – many actors finding it more rewarding than actually performing, which can become tedious after months in a long run. But ultimately, acting is a strange contradictory practice of being beholden to the character you are playing, and at the same time concentrated narcissistically on your own self as your essential tool for the job.

As an aside, I for one was always terrified of first nights. Some actors thrive on the adrenalin, but I simply found them an ordeal to be got through as quickly as possible. However, I was never quite as vulnerable as Laurence Olivier, who in his latter years was supposed to have dreadful stage-fright every time he ventured out into the spotlights.

Actors are often a vulnerable and discontented species.

Writing is quite different. It is creative, whereas acting is interpretive. It is ongoing, whereas acting is spasmodic. A writer can always write, but an actor can only act when he has a job. A writer is in charge of his life – he can live anywhere, travel anywhere, work anywhere – all he needs is his pen and paper, or laptop. An actor is dependent largely on outside factors.

The writer is also in total command of his work, whereas an actor is dependent on the script, the director, the rest of the cast, the vagaries of the production, and a myriad other elements. Of course these come into play when a writer's script comes to be performed, but during the creation of it he is the master. He is playing at God. He can create whole worlds, peopled with the beings of his imagination. He can dictate their doings, their feelings, their fates, and they can't dispute with him or answer back.

Furthermore, writing is an endless learning process, like learning to play the violin, or paint a portrait. It is not simply a matter of having great thoughts and jotting them down on paper. It is a question of turning those thoughts into something original and fascinating. A question of finding your own individual voice, and making your style unique (although I have to admit, many of the best selling novels today are written in a banal style that is anything but).

I may not have the finest technique there is, but I do know the value of constant honing and revision, which always, word by word, and sentence by sentence, improves the flow or the meaning of a passage. As Oscar Wilde put it: 'I spent all morning putting in a comma, and all afternoon taking it out again.'

One other aspect of the business is that the writer is in fact leading two lives at once. His real one, and that of his imagination. When one becomes tedious or problematic, he can slip into the other. And back again. Has a better way of coping with life's challenges ever been invented?

By the time of the *Chalk and Cheese* disappointment I had a fluctuating but fairly steady income from my various plays. *The Mating Game* in particular always seemed to pop up for a tour or summer season, just when we were wondering where the next money would come from. And subsequent comedies usually managed a turn in the reps and abroad.

Furthermore, I had reached the status as an actor where I could only accept reasonably strong or leading roles, which were of course fewer and farther between, thus paradoxically adding to the insecurity.

I persuaded Sheila, who was always initially reluctant to make a big change to our lives, that it would be better for us and for the children if we made the move to a more rural and less hectic environment, and if I concentrated on the steadier business of writing. We could also capitalise on the value of the Richmond house, and buy some nice country place, whilst still having something in the bank as reserve.

However, it didn't happen immediately. We spent many weekends, spread over a couple of years, exploring the classier country towns within reach of London – Henley, Windsor, Guildford, Reigate. We even went as far afield as Chichester, Haslemere and Oxford. However we eventually realised that these were all essentially commuter towns, still trapped by the tentacles of London, still bedevilled by busy traffic routes and packed station car parks. To escape London's suffocating embrace one had to travel a hundred miles.

I had always been drawn to the West Country – partly because of its mild weather and wild landscapes, partly because of childhood memories of holidays on harvest-time farms close to the glorious North Cornwall beaches, and partly because of the wealth of romantic literature spawned by those regions.

Cornwall and Devon were of course *too* far from London, which would always be my centre of operations as far as theatre productions were concerned. However, as an attractive halfway house between the West and the capital, lay the lovely city of Bath, with which I was slightly familiar, having toured there on various occasions. I remembered it as being a compact city, with stunning Georgian architecture, surrounded by wooded hills and rich farmlands. It was just over a hundred miles from London, and had a fast train service to there, as well as the M4 motorway.

We went to Bath to explore.

We were not to know that this decision would eventually get us more involved with the theatre world, with major stars, and with remarkable theatrical events, than had ever happened in London.

We discovered what was in effect a country town which one could easily walk across. Bath has a population of less than 90,000 citizens, closely accommodated within its superbly architectured terraces and crescents, all built in the golden Bath stone dug from its local quarries (though at that time somewhat sullied by weather wear and traffic fumes). It glowed with the history of its spectacular Roman Baths, its glorious Abbey, and its wealth of blue plaques recording the presence of such as Jane Austen, Charles Dickens, Sheridan, Beau Nash, Gainsborough, William Pitt, Nelson, etc, etc. It also had a beautiful setting, surrounded as it was by fields and wooded hills, with none of the sprawling industrial and commercial areas which bedevil the approach to so many townships.

We fell for it, and began surveying the local property scene. Our joint passion for nature and the countryside first led us to the various small villages surrounding the city, most quite unspoilt by time and the modern era. However, we soon realised that schooling for the girls would become a problem as they got older, since all the best schools were within the city's precincts, and would entail constant commuting to and from such. But these schools were all set in lovely surroundings on the various hills, and parts of Bath itself had a distinctly rural air, so we refined our search to the city itself.

After a couple of weekend trips from London we found a gracious Regency house set high on the Northern slopes of the city, with lovely South facing garden overlooking the green spaces of a park, towards the vista of roofs and spires in the city centre itself. One of the best schools was just around the corner. Sheila loved it as much as I did, which was a vital factor in persuading her to move.

The house needed some attention, but compared to the epic task of refurbishing our London home it would be a doddle. It was going to auction. By now we actually had an offer on the house in Richmond, which meant we could go for it.

And here I should digress to comment on the issue of estate agents.

Agents may have a general idea of house prices within their area, but when it comes to individual properties, especially distinctive ones, they know no more than does the owner. They react to it according to their individual tastes, which may be admiring or indifferent. And buyers will react likewise. It is all a question of finding the right one, who accords with one's own property tastes.

I had first approached a well-established firm of local agents, who came and inspected the Richmond house, made all the usual appreciative noises, and suggested a price just under £90,000. I considered this as probably reasonable, but a small voice whispered that perhaps we could do a bit better. I therefore went to a newly arrived, more modern agency, for their opinion. Two dashing young men in smart city suits came to view. They went round our large, but not especially magnificent abode, exclaiming profusely at its amenities.

Then they conferred briefly, and one of them said, "We think this is worth £125,000, and we could probably get it for you tomorrow."

I was stunned, and not a little sceptical. However they arrived the next day with a well-dressed couple speaking in upper class voices, who spent half an hour going round the house, and then said, "We love it. We'll give you the full asking price."

They turned out to be the Marquess of Londonderry and his wife, who had been searching for a London house for some time, and whose requirements were apparently met by ours. Not the sort of palatial home one would associate with the aristocracy, but presumably they had that back on their estate in Ireland.

There was almost a 40% difference between the two agents' estimates, which taught me a lesson I never forgot.

This marvellous outcome meant that we could go and bid for the house we had seen in Bath, and have plenty over to do it up with, whilst keeping a tidy sum in the bank to see us through our change in lifestyle.

Or so we thought.

Another lesson in property dealing. I had set an absolute limit of £90,000 on our auction bid for the place. I was confident we would get it, having studied the general cost of period houses in the city. But I had underestimated the rarity of such a detached house in such a setting. The bidding went way beyond our limit, and we hadn't even got a finger up.

We now had contracted to sell our home in London, but had nowhere else to live.

CHAPTER THIRTEEN

Extraordinary Developments

1980 was a difficult year. We had made the big decision to change our lives, but were now homeless, jobless, and directionless. Sheila especially was unhappy, being without a real home, and in a strange place with none of her friends or backup systems around her. She has also suffered the trauma of losing our third baby at birth, a tragedy which took us a long time to recover from.

The one advantage we had now, was that interest rates were at a historic high after the financial disasters of the 70s. So, with all the capital from our Richmond house sale earning interest in the bank, we at least had a steady income to keep us afloat.

We rented a small cottage in a hamlet near Trowbridge, some twenty minutes South of Bath, put the children into the village school (where a married pair of teachers, John and Flocky, became great friends), and set about house-hunting again.

It took us the best part of a year, scouring the city and the nearby countryside, but eventually we found a place that suited us. It was quite a large, sprawling Victorian villa high on Bath's southern slopes, next to a park. It was spacious, but chilly since it faced mainly North, but had a lovely walled garden with a stone summer house at one corner overlooking the city (which I later turned into a study to work in).

We commissioned an old acting friend, Richard Cornish – who had abandoned the unequal task of earning a regular living in the business, and had also moved to the Bath area, working as a very competent builder – to do the work we wanted on the place.

We found state junior schools for the growing girls, and set about investigating the social and cultural life of Bath.

Naturally our focus was mainly on the theatre facilities. The Theatre Royal, which I remembered from previous tours as being a beautiful but dilapidated venue, was closed, after the stage had virtually collapsed under the weight of a particularly heavy opera set. The city fathers were wrangling over whether to spend the large amount of money needed to restore this historic gem, or to demolish it altogether. Meanwhile the city had no theatrical events to celebrate, barring the odd amateur and fringe production.

I was by now busy writing my first novel, a far longer and weightier business than playwrighting. I wrote only in the mornings, since I had long ago discovered that four or five hours of such intense activity was the most the human brain could cope with.

To get ourselves out of the house, and reconnect with our traditional occupation, Sheila and I decided to mount a lunchtime production in a large converted chapel over the road from the Theatre Royal. We rounded up some of the local thespians and theatre enthusiasts, and put on a one act play I had written some years before, featuring Oscar Wilde and his wife Constance during the dramatic first night of *The Importance Of Being Earnest.* It was a piece in which I replicated much of Wilde's irreverent and witty style of speech, and I had always had a soft spot for it, but never managed to get the right production.

Sheila and I of course played the two leads (myself rather miscast as Wilde), and the modest audience for the couple of performances were extremely complimentary, but it was hardly a ground-breaking event. Nevertheless it had introduced us to a number of the people and institutions involved with the cultural scene of Bath, and had long term consequences.

Shortly afterwards, the Mayor of Bath launched an initiative to promote the arts in the city, and he held a meeting at the Guildhall, inviting anyone interested to come along and voice their opinions. We, and several others of the lunchtime company went. We found the main hall of the splendid Guildhall building thronged with perhaps two hundred people, who all seemed to know each other, talking animatedly together. They ranged from writers, to actors, to musicians, to art gallery owners, to museum managers, to simply interested local citizens.

The Mayor then invited people to come onto the stage and voice their suggestions through a microphone. Various offerings were listened to and applauded, and then the others in my group urged me forward, saying "Tell them what you think about the Festival."

I had from time to time voiced my feelings that the Bath Music Festival, whilst being one of the most prestigious in the country, was also somewhat elitist and snobbish, and lacked the vibrant fringe events that Edinburgh and other festivals had.

I went on stage and said as much. To my surprise the whole hall erupted with cheers and applause. I had evidently struck a chord.

The Mayor then said, "Well, there you are, Robin. Go ahead and do it."

I was landed.

I had no idea how to go about such a business, arts administration never having been one of my bents. However, I formed a small committee of a dozen people who were enthusiastic and knew the city, and we met together in our chapel performance space. We first of all discussed the various small venues around the town which would be suitable for fringe events. These seemed to be innumerable, varying from chapels and churches, to small theatres, meeting rooms and historic chambers.

I then said, "Well, we can't do anything unless we have funds to commission and publicise events. Seems to me we need at least a thousand pounds as seed money."

There was silence. No one there was either able or willing to put up cash for such a speculative venture.

Then a voice spoke from the far end of the table. "I'll give you the money."

It came from someone I hadn't noticed before, who had somehow slipped into the meeting. He was a fresh-faced young man, wearing a smart business suit and tie, in contrast to the scruffy casual attire of the rest of us.

His name was Christopher Shallis, and he turned out to be one of the most intriguing characters of my experience, as well as having a big influence on my future career. He was personable and charismatic. He ran a property company specialising in restoring old houses and buildings around the area, of which there were many. He had already become a millionaire before the age of thirty. He had an entrepreneur's talent for innovation, he drove a Porsche, and he was extremely sexually promiscuous (although it took me a while to discover this).

When I asked him why he had made the offer, he just said that it was in his interests to see Bath as a thriving tourist town.

With Christopher's thousand pounds, we were able to launch a few humble fringe events and lectures during the next Festival period. Then I applied for a grant from the city council for the following year, and managed to get a further five thousand, plus the use of a small office. I installed a paid part-time Administrator to take on the tedious work of hiring and organising venues, creating publicity and so forth, and we devised a more ambitious programme. This continued to expand into the busy Fringe Festival that exists today. I handed over the reigns fairly early on, as I had more compulsive aims.

One of them being to earn a living.

My sister, Elizabeth, and her surveyor husband, Peter, had returned from several years in the Middle East, where they had been involved in various career ventures. They first of all stayed in my mother's house in Richmond, with Liz's adopted son, Justin. However, with their several acquired skills, they were looking to start a business of their own together.

Out of sheer curiosity, I one day scanned the local Bath paper for commercial opportunities, and came across an advert for an antique furniture business in the nearby town of Frome. It was offering a complex of old buildings, including a shop with a large flat above, and several carpentry workshops at the rear, all for the price of £60,000. This seemed to me extremely cheap compared to London and Bath prices. I went to have a look.

I found a somewhat haphazard family firm, centred on buying and renovating period pine furniture, at that time popular as an alternative to more expensive mahogany and oak antiques. The business had quite a good turnover, and the shop and buildings had great potential. I rang Liz and Peter and told them to come and have a look.

They came down from London, inspected the outfit, and without any former experience in the furniture business, went for it.

I suggested that, instead of taking a bank loan to help with the purchase, Sheila and I should come in as partners, using some of our property nest egg. Together we bought it, and Liz and Peter moved into the very pleasant apartment above the shop, and set about learning the business – she running the financial side, whilst Peter, who had a brilliant practical brain, learnt furniture making.

Over the following years they first expanded the business, then bought us out, and then developed the company into quite a large enterprise, manufacturing new pine furniture from a much bigger factory premises in Frome. They still live close to the town, having sold out the whole venture, and invested the proceeds in various properties around the area.

My mother, who I have barely mentioned, moved down to a cottage in the town to be near us all. Mum had been through a life of various upheavals. She had divorced my father after twenty two years of marriage – more through incompatibility than anything else. She then married an engaging family friend named Kay, whose own marriage had broken up. Kay was very kind to us three teenage children, and he and my mother had fourteen happy years together. Then cultural differences finally intruded again. Kay, being a New Zealander, was desperate to live in the sun, and had built a modest villa by the sea in Ibiza. However Mother could not bring herself to leave the UK and her children, especially as my younger brother, Christopher, was having problems with depression. That marriage also broke up.

My mother now lived on her own, at first near us in Richmond, and later close to Liz and Peter in Frome. She eventually found some happiness, pottering around her small cottage garden, seeing her grand children, and lunching with the good friends she made locally. I visited her as often as I could, but as we spent more and more time abroad I'm afraid the onus of looking after her in her old age fell mostly on my sister and Peter.

My father, the self-made son of a Yorkshire butcher, meanwhile always maintained that he still loved her (he regularly sent her flowers on her birthday), but married twice more, and eventually ended up with his devoted wife Mary, in a large crumbling house on the edge of a Surrey golf course, where he spent his retirement chairing various rugby committees, going to Twickenham, playing golf with an assortment of colourful golfing friends, and spotting Royal Navy ships from their holiday apartment in an old Napoleonic fort overlooking Plymouth Sound. The family name is actually Oldroyd, but I took an earlier family name, Hawdon, as my stage name – why, I can't quite remember.

My family history has all the makings of an epic novel, but I'm not the one to write it.

Meanwhile, furniture making not being my metier, I still had to solve the problem of my future career.

The Theatre Royal had been saved for the city by the generous actions of a local businessman and philanthropist, Jeremy Fry. He was an inheritor of the Fry's chocolate fortune, and was now an industrial entrepreneur and inventor. He was also a great friend (and reputed lover) of Anthony Armstrong-Jones, who asked him to be best man at his wedding to Princess Margaret.

Jeremy purchased the Theatre Royal for £155,000, and set about raising the four million or so needed for the major restoration. He brought in top theatre architects, and the renowned theatre designer, Carl Toms, to do the work, and installed a young businessman, Crispin Raymond, to oversee the fund-raising project. Crispin, who was to become a great friend of ours, shared an office with another protégé of Jeremy's, inventor James Dyson, who would go on to become one of the world's richest men. James and his wife vied amicably with us later for the purchase of a lovely Bath house, which we couldn't really afford, but they could. They got it.

Jeremy Fry also commissioned Christopher Shallis and his property company, which by now was involved with large-scale developments such as new Sainsbury's stores, and station conversions, to manage the whole project.

After two years of work, the magnificently restored theatre – all gold leaf and chandeliers and hand-painted frescoes – opened to loud fanfares, with an opening performance by the National

Theatre of *Midsummer Night's Dream*, starring Paul Scofield (in my personal opinion the most magnetic actor of the late twentieth century), and attended by Princess Margaret. All of Bath fought for tickets.

The problem then, however, was how to run the place long-term. The venue was a touring theatre – as opposed to a repertory theatre, producing its own shows. It seated almost a thousand people within its classic Georgian auditorium, and was one of the major staging posts for productions on their way to London, or touring the country after a successful London run. The team who had raised the money and overseen the renovation were not experienced in commercial theatre, and after some months the programme of events did not look very exciting.

However, this was not my problem. I was at home, busily finishing my novel, and wondering how to get it published.

Then I received a phone call from Chris Shallis, who was of course on the theatre's board of directors. The conversation went something like this:-

"Robin, Jeremy Fry feels he has done his bit for the theatre, and wants to step down as chairman. He has asked me to take over."

I replied, "Great, Chris. You'd be terrific for the job."

"Yes, but I've said I will only do it if I can pick my own team, and my choice of Theatre Director."

"Quite right. You need to find new people."

"Do you think it would be easy to get someone good as Director?"

"Oh, yes. It's the most beautiful theatre in the country now. You'll have people falling over themselves to do it."

"I suppose I'd have to pay him quite a lot."

"Well, theatre salaries aren't the same as big business salaries."

"Do you think twenty thousand a year would be reasonable?"

"Yes, I think you'd get someone for that."

"Would you do it for that?"

Pause.

"Me?"

"Yes."

"No – I don't run theatres. I work on the other side of the footlights."

"Yes, but you've got experience of lots of theatres, and you know a lot of the London producers. You could do it."

I protested, "No, no – I'm a writer, not a theatre manager."

"Well, talk to Sheila, and take the weekend to think about it."

And he put the phone down.

My first reaction was to reject the idea out of hand. The plan was to live a quiet, semi-rural life turning out great works of literature and drama, far from the stresses of live show business.

But then I discussed it with Sheila, and we reassessed the situation. Firstly, this was an offer that would never come my way again – to run one of the most gorgeous theatres anywhere, with the choice of the most prestigious shows touring the country. Secondly it meant an actual salary for the first time in my life, not a minor consideration in our present circumstances, and certainly one which made Sheila's eyes light up. And thirdly – well, surely it couldn't be too difficult, and I'd still have time to carry on with my writing when off-duty.

Little did I know.

CHAPTER FOURTEEN

Theatre Royal Bath

I bought myself two business suits and several Marks and Spencer formal shirts, and went to meet the staff of the theatre.

The Theatre Royal (or TRB as it is commonly known) is much more than just a theatre. It occupies most of a city block, and has facilities that most others would envy. When I arrived, it already had a restaurant in the curving vaults beneath the auditorium, and a large entertaining suite high on the top floor. There were five spacious bars on the various different levels, a misshapen brick building at the rear, which used to be the scenery building block in the old days when the venue functioned as a repertory theatre, and various other adjoining under-utilised areas.

TRB was also virtually the only unsubsidised major theatre outside London, which was both an advantage and a disadvantage. It was free from any policy or bureaucratic interference from the Arts Council or the local councils, but it also meant that it had to stand on its own two feet. This status was under threat when I arrived, as the finances were not healthy. I initially had to fight hard to preserve it.

During my time there, with Chris Shallis's backing, I expanded the facilities by turning the rear scenery block into a studio performing space (which has developed over the years into the well-equipped Ustinov Studio, producing many ground-breaking new dramas); by bringing in a separate scenery building business to help facilitate the production of touring shows; by extending the entertaining suite into a luxury bar and lounge for the privileged fund-raising 'Friends' of the theatre (named the '1805 Club', that being the theatre's foundation year); and by installing a boutique Japanese restaurant in an unused space beside the stage door.

In later years, whilst I was still on the board of directors, the theatre took over the Garrick's Head pub which adjoined it, and also the small cinema complex at the rear, which has been turned into a busy theatre and activity space for young children named 'The Egg.'

The whole centre is still today a unique conglomeration of leisure and arts facilities, which is one of the glories of my home city.

However, that all came later.

On arrival I nervously installed myself in a room in the suite of offices high up within the block. This I shared with my inherited PA, Ann Meddings, who had been with the theatre all through the restoration and beyond, and knew everything about its workings and personnel. I was to depend on her hugely in the initial months.

I then called a meeting of all the staff, which we held in the Dress Circle as being the only space large enough. Including all the administration and marketing people, the backstage team, the box office and maintenance employees, and the part-time ushers and usherettes for performance times, there were over a hundred of them.

They were probably all rather sceptical about having someone with little managerial experience in charge. I introduced myself, gave a brief history of my theatrical experience, and told them that I would need all their help and advice in getting to grips with everything. I also said, with my fingers crossed, that now we had the most stunning theatre in the country, I wanted to bring to it the most stunning programme of events in the country.

As the days passed, and I gradually familiarised myself with the workings of the organisation, and with the complex business of booking shows and negotiating contracts, I began to relax and get into the swing of things. I realised that, after so many years in the business, and with experience of most of the provincial theatres in the land, in which I had either acted, directed, or had plays performed, I had unconsciously learned a lot about what theatre-goers want, and moreover what producers and performing companies want.

I knew well the actor's despondent feeling of arriving on a Monday evening at a provincial town, to find a darkened theatre, with no one there to greet you except for a dour stage door-keeper, who directed you through murky corridors to a tatty half-heated dressing room (backstage facilities are always the last to have money spent on them in cash-strapped theatres). I resolved that would not happen at Bath.

Our theatre was already quite busy at all hours of the day with extra-curricular activities, and moreover the dressing rooms had not been neglected during the renovation. They were well equipped and smart, and the star dressing rooms especially were magnificently decorated salons with silken drapes and chandeliers.

I began the tradition of having a theatre newsletter and welcoming message waiting on every artist's dressing table, which included an invitation to a first night drinks party, where they could say hello to audience members before scuttling off for dinner. These events were extremely popular with our patrons, if not always with the actors – but most of them were obliging, as it was a novel occurrence in their world, and they knew well the value of public relations.

I also made a point of personally going round all the dressing rooms before curtain up on the first night, and welcoming the cast to Bath, and to the theatre. I thus met up with a lot of old associates with whom I had worked over the years.

I next had to sort out the theatre staffing and programming, both of which were fairly haphazard. During my first few months there, I made myself unpopular in some quarters by firing one or two department heads who I felt weren't quite up to the job, rearranging the staff responsibilities in some areas, and rejecting the appeals of certain London managements who were eager to bring their rather undistinguished touring productions to Bath.

I knew that the success of the theatre was going to depend greatly on its marketing system. Again, when arriving at a provincial town, one could often hear the actors (and the producers) complaining loudly that they couldn't see any posters or publicity for their show about the place. I and the enthusiastic publicity department set about promoting TRB far and wide. We initiated a system of giving theatre lovers in outlying regions and villages free tickets, in exchange for distributing our posters and seasonal brochures around the pubs and shops in their area. We persuaded British Rail to let us put up a large illuminated signboard at the Bath Spa station, advertising the theatre to everyone who alighted from the London trains. We brought out a monthly newsletter (written mostly by myself) which gave information about all the forthcoming shows, as well as developments and special events within the theatre. We began a weekly 'Lunch and Listen' programme, in which patrons paid a modest amount for a lunchtime sandwich and glass of wine up in the 1805 rooms, whilst they listened to one of the stars of that week's show being interviewed about the production and their careers (again often by myself). These were always heavily oversubscribed.

And, most successful of all, we initiated the first ever subscription ticket scheme for weekly touring theatres, by which patrons got a successively increasing discount the more shows they bought tickets for. Everyone said at first that it couldn't be done, with such a fast changing and unpredictable tour programme around the country, but I was convinced that, with Bath's advantage in contracting the best available shows, we could produce a brochure for at least ten weeks advance booking, and could therefore offer the incentive of buying tickets for more shows than patrons would normally commit to. Furthermore they would be paying upfront, which would mean the theatre would always have a large reserve of cash in the bank.

The scheme became so popular that, not only did it considerably increase the number of seats sold, but it actually ended up providing well over half of all ticket income. I did have a few hairy moments, when I hadn't quite concluded a deal on a production before the printer's deadline on the next season's brochure, but we always got there in the end.

The other vital item for the theatre's finances was the catering side. Most theatres farm this out to catering firms, whose only interest is the easy exploitation of a captive clientele. I was determined to keep it in-house. Not only would the theatre retain all the bar and restaurant profits for itself, but it could also cross market between show tickets and restaurants, by giving discounts from one to the other. We brought in a catering manager to oversee the whole operation, installed a good chef, and did deals with wine merchants. The catering business brought the theatre over £100,000 a year during my tenure, worth three times that in today's money. I'm rather sad to see that catering firms have moved in since then.

But of course my most important duty was to bring in the shows that people wanted to see.

Those were the days before spectacular musicals dominated the London scene, when the touring business for plays, reviews and small-scale musicals was thriving. There was a constant stream of shows being tried out on the circuit before daring to face the critics in the West End, or of plays which had had a successful run in London, then embarking on a profitable run in the provinces. All interspersed by regular touring productions such as Oscar Wilde and Noel Coward classics, Agatha Christie whodunnits, and *Rocky Horror* or *Joseph And His Amazing Technicolour Dreamcoat* productions, with the occasional upmarket National Theatre or Royal Shakespeare Company offering thrown in.

However, filling over forty weeks of theatre a year (the pantomime season filled the rest) with appealing product was still a big challenge, and many less attractive dates struggled to achieve it.

I had the big advantage in that every management wanted to bring their show to beautiful and prosperous Bath, and to the newly renovated Theatre Royal, where good audiences were the norm, if not guaranteed.

I had a particularly productive relationship with a prolific London producer called Duncan Weldon. He and his business partner, Louis Michaels, had briefly owned the Theatre Royal some years previously, and he had a soft spot for it. He was also establishing a very profitable line of production, by which he brought over from America ageing film stars whose cinematic careers were on the wane, and putting them into well-tried classic plays for a UK tour, followed by a limited run in London.

Part of the art of persuading celebrities to embark on such a challenge, was to offer them the most attractive tour dates around the country – and for as many weeks as they would agree to, since the provincial profits could be substantial. Duncan discussed his plans with me, and wanted to make Bath his regular opening date for such shows. He could then sell the star the idea of coming to the famous historic city, staying in the luxurious Royal Crescent Hotel, and opening in the beautiful Theatre Royal.

This of course all added up to extremely expensive productions, which not many theatres could afford. However, as Duncan sold it to me, we could charge more for the tickets, and we would pick up extra income from the increased bar, restaurant, programme and ice cream sales that full houses would ensure. With fingers crossed again, I went for it.

Over the first year of my tenure we hosted shows starring Charlton Heston, Deborah Kerr, Peter O'Toole, Lauren Bacall, Anthony Hopkins, Liv Ulman, Vanessa Redgrave, Sarah Miles, and more. Later on came Al Pacino, Dustin Hoffman, Jack Lemon,

Maggie Smith... the list went on. The box office queues were down the street.

The theatre did indeed do well with such productions, although there were drawbacks. Some were so expensive that we only just broke even. The shows on either side of a starry vehicle were often more run-of-the-mill offerings, which would normally have pulled in decent audiences, but suffered badly after the outlay on such expensive tickets.

The stars too could be demanding. I got to know most of them to a greater or lesser extent, and the experience was revealing.

Lauren Bacall, still glamorous in her sixties, was extremely difficult to deal with, demanding two dressing rooms, private telephone line, special furniture, and – during dress rehearsals for the play – firing a number of dressers, hair stylists, and others who didn't satisfy her. She also caused minor mayhem by demanding that the Saturday evening performance be delayed, as it was too close to the matinée to allow her 'rest' period. The director, Harold Pinter, and I went together to her dressing room to try and persuade her, but she sent us packing like naughty schoolboys (something few could do to Pinter, who was an intimidating personality himself). She then had her Hollywood agent and lawyer on the phone to the producer, threatening to pull her out of the show. I was forced to give in to the demand, even though this resulted in a thousand theatre goers having at the last minute to reschedule their taxi bookings, restaurant times, baby-sitter arrangements, etc, etc.

However she gave a magnificent performance in Tennessee Williams' *Sweet Bird Of Youth.*

Charlton Heston, who visited the theatre twice, giving solid but uninspiring performances in *The Caine Mutiny Court Martial* and *A Man For All Seasons,* was a pleasant but humourless personality to meet. I did not spend much time with him, particularly as I disapproved strongly of his strident campaigning to preserve the insane American gun laws (he was later five-time president of the National Rifle Association). What is wrong with the USA?

Deborah Kerr on the other hand was a charming and gracious person, very like her on-screen presence. She attracted a great deal of unwelcome press attention when she could not remember her lines on the opening night of *The Corn Is Green.* What the press did not know was that, just prior to starting rehearsals, her long-time husband had announced that he wanted to live a separate life from her. Deborah was emotionally shattered by the news, but gamely continued to honour her contract. The show must go on.

The other star with whom I had strong contact was Anthony Hopkins (later Sir Anthony), whom I considered Britain's finest actor after the generation of Olivier, Gielgud and Scofield. His presence on stage was mesmerising, and he was a great loss to the theatre when he later abandoned it for ever for Hollywood (he later said he never enjoyed live performing).

The theatre always had a problem drawing in audiences during the hot summer months, and I was attempting to launch a prestigious 'Theatre Festival', which would appeal to the large numbers of summer tourists who flocked to Bath, and would hopefully launch starry productions with a West End future. Such an enterprise would require a big name to front it as Festival Director, and I had several discussions with Hopkins about the idea of him taking the role. The carrot was that he could have absolute control over the programme of three longer running plays, provided he either directed or acted in each of them. Anthony was initially quite excited about the project, and we discussed such plays as *Kean* (in which he had been superb on TV), and *Macbeth*, and various others.

Sheila proclaimed after a lunch with him, that he was one of the nicest men she'd ever met (partly, I suspect, because he strongly resembled her father). However, shortly after leaving Bath, Anthony was offered *King Lear* at the National Theatre, and the venture came to nothing.

Some time after I left TRB, Sir Peter Hall, past Director of both the Royal Shakespeare Company and the National Theatre, was persuaded to head up the summer festival, which he did for a number of years with great success.

A side issue to my running the theatre, was that I became marginally involved in Bath politics. TRB and its activities frequently came up in council discussions. It was also affected by the appalling Bath traffic system, which resulted in endless complaints from coach drivers and tourist organisers who couldn't find the building. I actually drew up a street plan myself, for a more efficient one-way circular system, as effected in other historic towns with narrow streets. It was published in the local paper, but came to nothing.

Through the theatre, I came to know both Jonathan Dimbleby and Chris Patten, Bath's MP, who were great friends together, and who lived locally. We socialised quite often, and Sheila and I and the girls joined their families for a few days one summer, at the same hotel in the Auvergne.

We had first met Patten, when invited to join him and his wife, Lavender, at dinner, by the Chairman of the Bath Conservatives. During an interesting evening talking local and national politics, I made the comment that I thought politicians were badly served by the media and the public, who seemed only interested in blaming them for all that was wrong with their worlds. I felt that most politicians were pretty intelligent and committed people doing a near impossible task.

Chris's wry comment was, "You obviously don't know enough politicians!"

He was a highly intelligent and effective one himself, and when he was ousted by a much inferior Liberal at the next election, the British Tory Party lost a potentially great future leader. He was wasted in the thankless role of Governor of Hong Kong.

After almost three years at the Theatre Royal, I felt I had done most of what I set out to do. I had gathered a really good team in all parts of the organisation, and the development of the theatre's facilities was virtually complete. I was also getting quite weary, as the job was virtually a twelve hours a day business. My idea of writing alongside was of course a pipe dream.

I began to hanker for my word processor and a quieter life. I told Chris Shallis that I wished to step down, but would not do so until I had found a good replacement. He was disappointed at my doing such a short term, but I agreed to stay on the Board of Directors, and began the search for someone else. I eventually approached an old friend, Stephen Barry, who had directed me in *Voyage Round My Father* at Cheltenham Rep, and was now running Farnham's

Redgrave Theatre. He was a repertory theatre man, but he didn't hesitate at the chance to take over at the Theatre Royal Bath.

CHAPTER FIFTEEN

Books and Golf and Sun

Meanwhile, other things had been happening in our lives.

We had sold our first rambling home in Bath, and had bought instead a tall semi-detached Victorian house, facing South West, high on the Southern slopes of the city. Summerhill House was reminiscent of our four story Richmond home, but had lovely sunny rooms with great views over Bath, and best of all, a lawned garden opening onto acres of National Trust fields and copses which stretched right to the city's edge. It also had an income producing flat, this time on the top attic floor.

We acquired a Border Collie pup from the RSPCA dog's home, who, being a sheep dog, required a lot of exercise, and we and the growing girls spent many hours roaming the adjoining countryside. Tammy, as our girl hound was called, was the most intelligent dog I have ever known, understanding dozens of different words, and living as an adored member of the family – along with various cats, hamsters, and other species – to the astonishing age of twenty one.

The position of this house also gave me a delightful walk into the city each morning whilst I was at the theatre – down a steep footpath through the fields, along the towpath of the Kennet & Avon canal, over a bridge of the River Avon, and thence to the stage door. It took twelve minutes. Coming home in the evenings after a long day took a bit longer! But it kept me fit.

Financially, we were doing quite well for once. I not only had my twenty thousand salary from the theatre, but I had also sold my first novel, which I had finished just prior to taking up the TRB post.

This was an epic nature story, in the same vein as *Watership Down,* about a war between two colonies of ants, and titled *A Rustle In The Grass.* The Cold War between Russia and the West was at its height, and the parallel was not hard to miss.

At first I had trouble finding a publisher, ants not being as seductive as rabbits. But then I found a semi-retired literary agent who lived near Bath (ironically on the Longleat estate, where he was quite friendly with eccentric Viscount Weymouth, previously mentioned). This was Nicholas Thompson, who had been a top London literary agent in his time, and still had contacts there. He managed to get a deal with Hamlyn books, a subsidiary of Hutchinson. They said they loved the book, but in order to sell it would need to persuade all the management team to make it their 'Book Of The Month', which would give it the extra publicity needed. This they did, and paid me £15,000 advance, which was not a bad sum in those days.

The history of *A Rustle In The Grass* is interesting. I think it sold most of its sixty thousand first print run, but never really took off into the best seller lists, despite some great reviews. This was of course all before the Amazon and Kindle revolution, which has both expanded and devastated the book business. However, years later, when that upheaval was well under way, we discovered that the novel had gradually acquired a list of five star reader reviews on Amazon, especially in the USA, although how it had spread there I'm not sure. These included phrases such as, "*... a fantastic, beautifully told story that grows on you the older you get.*" "*...by far the best fiction book ever written*"(!) "*...my favourite book until this day. My teacher borrowed it, and two years later there were twenty copies on the classroom shelf for all the students to read.*" etc, etc.

On the strength of these, the book was later republished in the UK by Thistle. It has still never taken off into the stratosphere, but I keep hoping.

Sheila's working life had meanwhile developed over the years through numerous stages. Having gradually abandoned her acting career because of children and house moves, she then taught drama, and directed amateurs in schools and prisons(!), she became a marriage-guidance counsellor, a writer herself, and finally a fully fledged professional psychotherapist, with her own consulting rooms in our various houses. This gave her much experience of the human condition, a fund of stories both tragic and hilarious, and contributed considerably to our finances.

With our more secure economic status (we still had money in the bank from our various property ventures), we began to think of buying a holiday home.

I have always hankered for the sun. Ever since my early childhood during the dark and chilly war years in Newcastle-on-Tyne, when my father was away with the Royal Artillery, I have been greatly affected by warmth and sunlight. I don't actually succumb to SAD, since unhappiness is not in my nature, but there is no doubt that my spirits sink a little when winter approaches, and lift when the sun comes out. Sheila is not quite as addicted as I am, having been conditioned by her childhood in the wet and wild farmlands of Wales, but as she grew older she too acquired an attachment to the sunshine.

During my teens, I and my younger brother and sister, spent many a blissful barefoot holiday at our step-father's villa on the island of Ibiza, still a relatively unspoilt and sparsely inhabited Mediterranean island. There, we learned to surf and sail and water-ski, and it instilled in me a love of sun and warm waters that has never left me. I even thrive in tropical climes, when most people are wilting with the heat. (Sheila and I actually spent Christmas 2019 at Uluru/Ayers Rock. The outside temperature hit 50C on Christmas Day. That is HOT!)

I had always felt in my heart that, circumstances permitting, I would one day wish to live in a warmer climate than the British Isles offered.

After quite a lot of research, and the experience of various holiday and location trips around Southern lands, we settled on the Canary Islands as having the best year-round climate, within easy reach of the UK, and where property was still relatively cheap. I was also influenced by memories of my time filming *Dinosaurs* on two of the islands, with their wide sandy beaches and cactus dotted mountainsides. The Canaries are a four hour flight from Britain, and lie off the Western coast of Africa parallel with the Sahara Desert, but because of their position in the Atlantic Ocean the climate is maritime, and so benign almost all the year round, with over three hundred days of sun.

The other requirement for a holiday retreat was that it should have access to good golf courses.

Another digression. I had always played a sport of some kind. I had been quite a good rugby player at school (though never as good as my father, who captained Richmond Rugby Club in his time, and came close to playing for England). However at eighteen, I tore a knee cartilage badly in a game, and that ended my rugby career. Once I was established in London I took up squash, which is a fabulous game for getting strenuous exercise in a brief space of time. I continued to play that after coming to Bath, but after my old knee injury had brought me low several times, the doctor told me to give the game up, or it would cripple me for life. So I then took up golf, a sport I had briefly dallied with in my teens, but never had the time for since.

Golf is the most extraordinary game on the planet. Notwithstanding its expense, it's the most popular sport ever invented. Those who dismiss it as 'a good walk spoiled' have no idea of its remarkable features. It is the greatest combined challenge to both mind and body that I know. If one is not 99% focussed on that silly little ball and your body's relation to it, it will never go where you want it to. I can think of no other activity that requires such a degree of concentration. The complexities of the golf swing, and of interpreting the lie of the land and the effects of sun, wind, and other factors on the ball's flight, are endless. My wonder at the astonishing skills of the top professional golfers is unbounded.

Furthermore, it is the most companionable and eco-friendly of all sports. It is virtually the only major one where you aren't trying to blast your opponent off the pitch, and where curtesy and convivial talk are all part of the ethos, however fierce the competition. Many great friendships are initiated on golf courses. It is also excellent exercise, since one walks around six miles during the course of a game, up hill and down dale. You rarely see an obese person on a golf course, except in America, where many clubs ludicrously insist on one riding a golf buggy.

And you can play it until you have one foot in the grave.

Furthermore, golf takes place in some of the most beautifully cultured and nature-abounding spaces on the planet. I often think of golf courses as being the modern equivalent of Capability Brown landscapes – rolling green pastures, magnificent trees, and tranquil lakes – all teeming with animal and bird life such as you find in few other places.

As I investigated the Canary Islands, I discovered that they had several championship courses under construction to cater for the expanding tourist trade. One in particular caught my attention. It was advertised as being in the south of the largest island, Tenerife – on a wide open location undulating down to the sea, close to the airport, and with a cluster of villas under construction around its fairways.

I went on a weekend exploratory trip (curtesy of the Spanish tourist department), and found a superb course already completed, with various holiday complexes and hotels going up around the fringes. It was called Golf del Sur.

One site there appealed to me. A terrace of half a dozen linked villas, on the edge of a complex with a large communal swimming pool. The position was bang in the middle of the golf course, looking straight out over one of the wide fairways to the sea. Construction of the six houses themselves had not yet begun. Consequently the off-plan price was very reasonable.

I put down a deposit.

Thus began a twenty year affair with Tenerife that brought joy, drama, and problems in almost equal measure.

CHAPTER SIXTEEN

Tenerife

Tenerife is a fascinating island. The largest of the Canaries, being roughly sixty miles long by forty wide, it is really one gigantic semi-dormant volcano. Mount Teide, at over twelve thousand feet, is the highest mountain in all Spanish territories. The summit can be seen from all parts of the island, and even in mid-summer there is sometimes snow there, which contrasts with otherworldly fields of black clinker from its last eruptions during the nineteenth century. The Southern slopes, where most of the tourist industry gathers, have a dry climate and a strange barren beauty. The only vegetation is scrub and cactus, broken by the lines of palm trees and forests of bougainvillea planted around the resorts. The North is wilder and wetter, with mountain spurs and valleys descending from Teide's summit, as spectacular as anything in the lower Alps.

Santa Cruz, the capital, is a sea port with some fine Spanish architecture, an opera house, and several grand period style hotels. The island has a long history, being a staging post between Europe and the Americas, and the Far East routes round the Cape of Good Hope. Spain has always retained ownership, despite assaults from other empires, particularly Britain, which was repulsed at the Battle of Tenerife, in which Nelson lost his arm.

It is also, as we were to discover, a favourite refuge for pirates, smugglers, crooks and swindlers from all corners of the planet, encouraged perhaps by an incurably corrupt streak in the indigenous Spanish temperament.

We took possession of our first ever holiday home, and for the next twenty years or so the family travelled to the island two or even three times a year for some glorious sunny holidays, the length of stay increasing as time went by.

I was able to keep writing whilst there, having a lot more free time, especially as the girls were now weekly boarding at Kingswood, one of Bath's fine private schools (another financial gamble!).

Both Sheila and I took up golf with some seriousness, joining the Golf del Sur and Bath golf clubs. I began playing two or three times a week, and my game improved considerably. I was a competent, but never a great golfer. I briefly got my handicap down to ten, but never managed to creep into single figures, the ultimate goal for all aspiring amateurs.

We explored the island, discovering interesting mountain villages, and superb restaurants run by immigrant chefs from many nations. We made friends with some of the ex-pat British residents who had made their homes there, and found a surprisingly lively cultural life, with regular concert and opera events taking place.

And we also began to discover the dark side.

The king of crime in Tenerife was a man named John Palmer, notorious for being the brains behind the record-breaking Brink's Mat gold robbery. Coincidentally he had lived just outside Bath, and the stolen gold ingots, worth some twenty six million pounds, had been melted down in an outbuilding on his estate, although he escaped conviction by claiming that he was unaware of the process! His links to the London and international crime worlds, to police corruption, and to numerous gangland kidnappings and murders were legendary. He was reputed to be worth £300 million, and as the Brink's Mat investigations rumbled on, had fled to Tenerife in his private jet, where he set up a huge property racket, laundering Columbian drug money through tourist developments, and then mis-selling timeshares in those to gullible holiday-makers. He was eventually imprisoned for his timeshare frauds, and years later murdered with a shotgun by persons unknown. Few mourned his demise.

Meanwhile his tentacles had spread all over the island, involving numerous cases of terror, intimidation, and murder, mostly within his own criminal circle.

We eventually found ourselves drawn into the shady aspect of the island's activities. Encouraged by the pleasant style of life there, and by the booming tourist industry, and needing to invest our modest nest egg of savings, we bought two more properties on the growing golf complex – a small holiday apartment in an exotic new block, and a bare office/business suite in another development. The theory was that these would provide income whilst growing in value.

The business space disappointed when the tenants, a hairdressing salon, stopped paying the rent and had to be evicted. The holiday apartment proved far more problematic.

For a year or so all went well, with regular lettings more than covering the costs. Then fell the bombshell. We, and every other owner of the three hundred-plus apartments on the development were issued with demands from the Spanish bank to pay back an average of £30,000 per property, which was outstanding on the developer's loan, and about which no one had been informed.

It subsequently transpired that the practice in Spain's construction industry was for builders to take out large mortgages to erect their projects, and to cover the repayments with the cash flow from the sale of the individual units as they were completed. This is common across the planet, but in Spain's huge tourist business it is more excessive than elsewhere. All is fine of course whilst economies are growing and leisure industries are flourishing. Developers rush to get on the bandwagon. But when a downturn comes, sales of such properties dry up, and they are left with a cashflow crisis. In the Canaries, and all along the Costa del Sol and Spain's other resort areas, this boom and bust cycle was exaggerated by Spain's lax money controls and corrupt systems.

We were fortunate in that most of the proprietors on our complex were British. I and three others who were there when the news exploded, formed a committee and called a meeting of all the owners. We got agreement from everyone to create a fighting fund with a donation from each owner of a thousand pounds (this was before the euro was created). We then hired a top lawyer from Madrid to investigate the situation.

We discovered that ours was not a unique case. All over Spain, developers experiencing hard times were in league with the banks and the local lawyers doing the conveyancing, to conceal the loans from purchasers until their cash flow picked up. When that didn't happen, the developer would go bankrupt, and the bank would then call in the loans on all the individual properties. At that time, many thousands of Britons, some of whom had invested their life savings in their dream of a retirement in the sun, lost everything to the system.

Over the course of the next five years, through endless court cases and appeals, our lawyer was able to prove the complicity of the banks and the local solicitors in our particular case, and got the mortgages lifted. Several bank directors resigned, and various lawyers were disbarred. We breathed a sigh of relief and sold our apartment as quickly as possible. Others were not so lucky.

Our Madrid lawyer himself had demanded his £250,000 fee in cash. I and the committee had to arrange it from a London bank, and were present when he picked the money up, and trotted off down Piccadilly with it in a large brief case! It would have served him right if he'd been robbed on the way.

However he did the business.

Despite all that, we have wonderful memories of Tenerife, where we were to spend more and more time. We sold the villa, and converted the problematic business space into a lovely apartment with large sun terrace and sea views, and escaped the British winters there for months at a time.

But eventually, as we got older, and thoughts turned to where we might eventually want to retire, we decided that the corrupt and often uncouth Spanish society was not permanently for us.

We began to consider the more civilised and stylish culture of the South of France.

CHAPTER SEVENTEEN

Don't Dress For Dinner

Apart from all that, having left the Theatre Royal, I still had to think about procuring an income.

I had not written anything for three years, and the earnings from all my old plays were drying up. I did make a brief return to acting when, out of the blue, Salisbury rep offered me the part of Henry Higgins in Bernard Shaw's finest play, *Pygmalion* (the role which Rex Harrison made famous in the musical version, *My Fair Lady).* I had an enjoyable time doing this great part, opposite Anita Dobson of *East Enders* fame as Eliza Doolittle. But it didn't solve anything long term. It was my final acting performance.

In some desperation I first contemplated going into the Tenerife property business myself, and then becoming a theatrical agent when Richard Stone offered me a partnership in his agency, after I had briefly stood in for someone in his office ("I will make you a millionaire in five years", he said). Thankfully I pulled back from both before committing to such mad ideas.

I then made what turned out to be probably the most vital phone call of my career.

Mark Furness was a London producer who had mounted a number of my plays over the years – on tour, in summer seasons, and in rep. We together had a near miss with a comedy titled *French Farce* (later *There's A Small Hotel...*) which he staged with a view to a West End showing. It was inspired by the Richard Burton/Elizabeth Taylor tempestuous on-off marriage previously mentioned. I had always been a fan of the hilarious Charlie Chaplin/Buster Keaton/Harold Lloyd style of physical comedy, and had conceived this as a Feydeau style farce containing as many physical jokes as possible, ranging from soda-water soakings, to cream cake smotherings, to revolving door trappings, to lift shaft disasters. We got a great cast, including Patrick Cargill as a harassed French hotelier, prone to outrageous malapropisms ("Zey are inspecting my wife's rear quarters," and "I will be happy to go to my incestors", and "I will have you ejaculated from ze hotel!"), and Sylvia Syms, the beautiful star of *Ice Cold In Alex* amongst others, as the Elizabeth Taylor character. The cast was athletic and the set was huge, being two stories high and incorporating a staircase and a fully working lift, both of which played a large part in the mayhem. I was extremely happy with the production, and during a laughter provoking tour thought I might have another West End hit to follow *The Mating Game*. However it turned out that there were no London theatres available, large enough to accommodate the set, and although Mark extended the tour for as long as possible whilst waiting, none came free in time and the show ended. The play has since been done in various foreign countries, but it was one of the big disappointments of my career.

Now, in my perplexity as to what to write next, I rang Mark, and asked him for advice as to what the theatre business was looking for at the present time.

Mark said, "Funny you should call now. I've just bought an option on a French comedy by Marc Camoletti, and was wondering what to do with it. Would you like to have a look at it?"

Camoletti was a prolific Paris based author of French farces, including the highly successful *Boeing Boeing*, which had played all over the world (and still does).

I jumped at the chance, and read the text and the rough English translation that Mark had commissioned. The French title was *Pyjamas Pour Six*, and it involved the usual complex shenanigans between husbands, wives, mistresses, lovers and others in an almost unintelligible plot. The great thing about it was the opening situation.

All comedies and farces have to begin with a crisis of some sort. If that crisis is sufficiently urgent and complex to provide ongoing ramifications that can be developed over two hours, then you have a play. There are of course only so many crises worthy of dramatising, and they all involve either sex, money, or wrongdoings of one sort or another.

The crisis of *Pyjamas* was the not very original one of an unfaithful husband with an unfaithful wife, each of whom was keeping their affair secret from the other. However it had a particularly ingenious opening predicament. What happened after that became rather confused and rambling, as happens with many French plays, but the piece seemed to me to have potential.

I asked Mark how much of a free hand I would have with the adaptation. He said that it was some time since the play's run in Paris, so there should be quite a bit of leeway.

As I started writing, I tried to stick as close as possible to the original plot line. However its inconsistencies kept getting in the way, and gradually the play started to take on a life of its own. Over the course of a frantically creative three weeks, which included Christmas Day, it practically 'wrote itself', and I delivered it to Mark at the beginning of the new year, 1990.

We deliberated a lot over the title (always one of the most problematic items for a new play), and I eventually came up with *Don't Dress For Dinner*, whose alliteration and vague sexual intimation were more appealing than *Pyjamas For Six*. The play opened in London a year later with a cast of well-known, but not major star faces, including Simon Cadell, Su Pollard, Jane How, and John Quayle. They were all brilliant. The reviews were nearly all good, and some were raves (*"I thought this would be boring boring, but it isn't isn't." "Hurtling along at the speed of light, this breathtaking farce is a near faultless piece of theatrical invention."*) The show ran for six years, the last of the long running comedies before the musical tsunami completely engulfed the West End.

This play transformed our fortunes and opened up a whole new second phase of my writing career. Mark Furness had strong contacts with American producers, in particular a wonderful man called James McKenzie, who ran three of the most active US regional theatres, near New York, Chicago, and San Francisco. He was President or Vice President of numerous theatrical bodies. James mounted *Don't Dress For Dinner* at his prestigious summer festival at Green Bay, north of Chicago, and I was invited to attend the rehearsals and first night there.

I found a beautiful site amongst the trees on the shores of Lake Michigan, where a large complex of barns had been transformed into a spacious theatre, scenery block, rehearsal space, and restaurant, with living accommodation for the company (and their families) in log cabins dotted around the woods. The festival was known for its idyllic summer ambience and high production standards, and actors from the strong Chicago theatre population were all eager to join the 'Peninsular Players' as the company was called.

This was the start or a long association with James McKenzie and the summer seasons on Green Bay, where over the years half a dozen of my plays have been performed, and where I, and sometimes Sheila too, visited regularly.

It was also the launchpad for many of my repertoire of titles in the United States, which I had hitherto never managed to conquer. *Don't Dress For Dinner* went on to play most of the stock (repertory) and amateur theatres across America with great regularity, and still does. It reached Broadway at the American Airways Theatre on 42nd Street in 2012, but despite being nominated for Best Comedy at the Tony Awards, the production was not as good as the London one, and the show only ran for five months.

The text was published by Samuel French, the world's biggest publishers of stage plays, whose lists are regularly scoured by repertory and amateur companies everywhere, and this guaranteed publication of many of my later plays. All my most successful comedies are now published, which helps enormously with their proliferation.

There is an aftermath to the story. We had only managed to obtain the English-speaking rights to Marc Camoletti's play, he and I splitting the royalties. During the West End run, and its subsequent productions across America, Canada, Australia and elsewhere, enquiries began to come in from theatres and producers in Europe and other foreign countries, for the rights to produce *Dinner* in their own languages. However Camoletti, by now aware of the large differences between his play and my version, refused to grant permission. As the requests grew into a deluge, we tried over many years to get him to relent, but he refused, saying that they had to use the original *Pyjamas Pour Six* instead, which few wanted to do. This situation has continued long past his death, and his estate still refuses to give permission.

As a fellow author, I can understand his resentment at what happened with his work. However, after so many years during which it has faded into obscurity in France, and after the loss of probably several hundred thousand pounds in royalties to each of us, one would have thought that pride would give way to practicality. My agent is still trying.

CHAPTER EIGHTEEN

Weddings and God

Inspired by the premise of *Dinner*, I next wrote a comedy using vaguely the same trick, but in a very different context. I had always felt that there was a good farce to be written around a wedding day, as opposed to the many romantic comedies on the subject. The problem was how to create it, and where to set it without involving a large cast, since most producers look to pay no more than half a dozen main salaries.

I then lighted on the idea of setting it in the bridal suite of a honeymoon hotel on the morning of the wedding itself. The opening crisis situation was simple. The groom wakes up in the honeymoon bed with a hangover from the previous stag night, a strange girl in bed beside him, and the bride-to-be about to arrive. I had the circumstance, but no idea where it would go from there, as is usually the case with my work.

Again the play 'wrote itself' and the end result was *Perfect Wedding*, which was to bring me another huge disappointment, but also more productions world-wide than even *Don't Dress For Dinner.*

A successful agent turned producer, Michael Linnit, got very enthusiastic about the piece, and set it up for a London production.

He gathered a great cast, including members of the popular TV comedy series *Men Behaving Badly,* and managed to get the three most important try-out theatres, Windsor, Guildford, and Bromley, all involved in the production. I again thought I had a winner.

Then, only a few weeks before we were due to start rehearsals, the Theatre Royal at Windsor, which was building the set, and where the show was to open, declared itself bankrupt and closed its doors.

The malign gods of the theatre had struck again. A rare chance to get another comedy into the West End was lost, probably for ever.

However, by now a lot of people had got interested in the play, enticed especially by its title and subject matter, and it gradually gathered momentum in a number of places, at home and abroad.

The splendid Mill at Sonning dinner theatre, which was, and still is, one of the last theatres to keep up the tradition of British stage comedy, put it on for a successful run. A new young production company ran a poorly produced and not so successful UK tour. The Peninsular Players at Green Bay put it into their next summer season. Theatres in Germany, Scandinavia, Poland, Israel, and Russia (my first foray into that country), translated it and mounted productions. Samuel French published it, amateur companies took it up with enthusiasm, and its reputation slowly spread. Since the Windsor debacle *Perfect Wedding* has had several hundred productions in over thirty countries, it has been filmed or televised in various foreign languages, and there have been attempts by film producers in both Britain and Hollywood to mount an English film version.

How it might have fared had the West End production materialised we will never know.

But the failures of *The Hero, There's A Small Hotel* and *Perfect Wedding* to reach London were not my only such experiences. I had already suffered yet another big disappointment in that area. Some time previously I had written my only produced musical. Titled *Love Match*, it was a small-scale show in the Stephen Sondheim tradition, recounting the turbulent ups and downs of an ordinary middle class family. It had beautiful music by Nola York, and went on at Windsor Theatre Royal. Again I had reviews that writers dream about:–

> *'This is a gem of a show and one which deserves a much wider showing...' 'Few shows in the last few years have brought such professional and perfectly constructed entertainment to the stage...' 'Not since Sondheim's COMPANY have marital problems and modern pressures been better served in a musical...'*

Once more I thought I had a hit, but the London managements, all on the look out for the next Lloyd Webber spectacle, showed no interest, and it folded after the Windsor run.

I don't think I'm being unrealistic when I say that I've had my fair share of bad luck.

However, the twin experiences of *Dinner* and *Wedding* led on to a number of other comedies, most of which have had regular foreign productions scattered across the globe, encouraged greatly by my theatre agent of the last fifteen years, Brendan Davis. America, with its plethora of theatres in almost every town and village, is of course a huge market. In Germany I have a great producer/director,

Horst Johanning, who has launched many of my comedies at his Contra-Kreis Theatre in Bonn. Poland, which has an illustrious theatre tradition, always has half a dozen Hawdon plays running at any one time, thanks largely to my wonderful Polish translator, Ela Wozniak, who knows every producer in the country. We regularly visit both those countries to attend premieres. My comedy *Shady Business* had a five month run with a starry cast at the lovely Michodière Theatre in Paris. Sheila and I went to the premiere, sitting between one of Gerard Depardieu's wives/partners and veteran star Claude Brasseur, whose family members were in the company.

I am now better known abroad than at home.

All this has been fine, and solved our financial worries for the next thirty years. We were never wealthy, but we had a comfortable lifestyle, and could choose to travel and live more or less wherever we wished. However, I still craved recognition as a serious writer.

During my last year at Theatre Royal Bath, the annual Booker Prize – recognised, along with the Pulitzer Prize, as being one of the world's foremost literary awards – was won by Kingsley Amis with his *The Old Devils*, a semi-autobiographical tale of boozing and womanising in the South of Wales. I had laughed a lot at the early book that made his name, *Lucky Jim,* but never thought his later novels reached the same level of audacious hilarity. *The Old Devils*, however, did have an intriguing sprawl of a narrative, and wonderful eccentric characters. Under the auspices of the embryonic production company I had launched at the theatre, I approached Amis's agent to ask if he would be interested in a stage adaptation of the novel. As a carrot I suggested we could approach a top dramatist to do the job. Kingsley agreed, and I then went to two or three big names – Willy Russell, Tom Stoppard, Simon Gray – with the idea. They all, one after the other rejected it, being occupied with their own projects. So, with some trepidation, I suggested via the agent that I write it myself.

The author replied that he would need to meet me to hear my ideas. He invited me to lunch at his home.

Kingsley Amis (later Sir Kingsley) was then in his sixties, and had a fearsome reputation as a boozer, a womaniser, and the angriest of the angry young men generation. He was also the reluctant father of Martin Amis, arguably as notable a chronicler of his own times. Kingsley was living on his own, but in an apartment in the house of his first wife (divorced) and her husband, who saw that he was fed and looked after. How that arrangement came about was the subject of much gossip.

I went to lunch in a state of some apprehension.

He met me at the door of the nice Regency house in Primrose Hill – a large, red-faced man with, if I remember correctly, greying hair and conventional British tweed jacket and corduroys. He seemed amiable enough, and when he suggested opening a bottle of Perrier Jouet champagne before lunch, I could hardly refuse. However, he himself soon graduated to Black Label Johnny Walker whiskey, and my nerves increased, knowing his reputation for abruptly losing his temper when in his cups.

All went well, and we spent several hours discussing my ideas for dramatising his book – myself rationing my intake of champagne, he drinking twice as much whiskey, though whether that was less than his usual intake I couldn't say.

The upshot was that I wrote the play – quite a task, as it was a lengthy book, involving many colourful characters and a wide array of locations. I sent it to Kingsley for his approval. He made certain suggestions, but then gave the go-ahead and went back to his bottle. I then brought in the Theatre Clwyd (the unofficial National Theatre of Wales) and the Prospect Company as co-producers, with Toby Robertson as director. Toby was a dear, amiable, but slightly disorganised man (his rambling London house was almost as dilapidated as our Richmond one before I restored it). He had directed me years before in *The Importance Of Being Earnest.* Now, he made a good job of the casting, and we started rehearsals.

I soon realised that the play was too long. I had harboured doubts as I wrote it, but wasn't sure how fast the pace would be, so unwisely left it until the rehearsal period to decide how much needed editing. Big mistake. I should have known that actors, once into their roles, hate having to lose lines.

By the time the cast had expanded bits of business and paused for laughter, the running time in rehearsals was over three hours. I suggested to Toby that we needed three quarters of an hour taking out. He agreed. Overnight I made the cuts. Toby put it to the cast the next day. Then the protests began.

"Oh, that's my best speech, you can't cut that!"

"Oh, but my whole character depends on that bit!"

"Oh, but I won't be on for twenty minutes if that scene goes."

Etc, etc... And Toby was not the ruthless director who would insist on having his way.

We managed to cut about twenty minutes from the play, but it was still too long. It went on tour and garnered very respectful notices and audience reactions, but I knew that another chance had been missed for a real success.

Then I attempted something more ambitious.

At the end of the eighties, the brilliant but crippled scientist Stephen Hawking had written his best-selling book, *A Brief History Of Time*. Public interest in space and astronomy had increased enormously since the first Sputniks, the American moon landing, and various Mars probes. In his book Hawking set out to explain modern scientific thinking in layman's terms, accessible to the man in the street. It sold millions of copies, and is still reputed to be the most widely bought book that readers have never finished!

However, Hawking did the job brilliantly, explaining in plain English, not only Newtonian and Einsteinian physics, but also delving into the mysterious hidden world of quantum mechanics. The publisher had told him that every mathematical formula he put into the book would halve his sales, so there were none. Hawking's ultimate conjecture was that one day science would discover the 'Theory of Everything', combining all conflicting hypotheses into one gigantic Eureka moment.

I have always been intrigued by the science of the universe, not only through the usual fascination with the stars and their courses, but also from a philosophical aspect. I believe implicitly in the Darwinian theory of evolution as opposed to superstitious and religious speculations.

I read *A Brief History Of Time* and was enthralled by it. I am no advanced mathematician, but I understood the broad concepts of what Hawking was explaining, although I have to admit that the second part, which went into nuclear science and the various theories of quantum electrodynamics, had me floundering somewhat. But then advanced scientific brains still flounder over all that today.

I began to wonder whether there was a stage play that could be written around the subject, in the way that Michael Frayn had explored early nuclear investigations in his piece *Copenhagen* (although I have always found that play something of a prolonged history lesson).

I conceived the idea of basing Hawking's explanations around the dramatic story of his own life, which involved the diagnosis at an early age of motor neurone disease, his subsequent battles with his slowly accumulating disablement, his marriages, and his growing worldwide fame.

Over many absorbed months of work I eventually produced a play. I had done more research and revision than I have ever done, gradually condensing the scientific explanations into intelligible, and often comic speeches, and fitting them into a dramatic form.

The cast consisted of only three main characters – Stephen himself, his wife Jane, and God. It was God who was the main driving force behind the story – announcing from the start that one of the evening's objectives was to decide whether he existed or not. Meanwhile he brought to life the notable characters in Stephen Hawking's own life, with his impersonations of early professors and scientists, Newton and Einstein, the Pope, and even the Queen! A lot of quick changes were involved, along with jokes about him having many guises, and crafty ways of manipulating humanity.

Soon after finishing the play I received a phone call from

Danny Moar, who was now running Theatre Royal Bath, as well as the successful production company attached to it.

"I hear you've written a play about Stephen Hawking," he said.

"Yes."

"I'd like to have a look at it."

The upshot was that Danny mounted the play, bringing in Jonathan Church as director, and after the usual protracted search for a cast, got Robert Hardy, well known for his Churchill impersonations, to play God, and Stephen Boxer for Hawking. The setting was bare, but bounded by a huge cyclorama, onto which were projected spectacular images of the heavens, as well as depictions of the various locations involved.

I had also sent the text to Stephen Hawking himself, via his Cambridge college, as a cautionary measure, for his sanction. It came back from one of his assistants with the necessary approval. However, during the following year whilst we organised the production, he went through a dramatic time in his life, divorcing his wife Jane, and marrying his chief nurse, who largely had control over all his daily activities.

The press had by now found out about the production, and went to him for his opinion. He, or more probably his new wife, now stated that he did not approve of his life being staged in such a way (although he did not object much later to a film being made about him). This attracted quite a lot of publicity.

We opened in Malvern to what seemed enthusiastic audience reception, and to approving local notices. Robert Hardy, after initial difficulty learning his huge part, increased in confidence, and Stephen Boxer was brilliant as Hawking in all the stages of his life. The tour went well, and came to Bath, where all our friends and family attended, and the accolades continued. Then came the bombshell.

A few London critics, alerted by Hawking's publicised comments, went prematurely to view the play at Oxford. Two of the most important ones supported his view of it, and one in particular, Charles Spencer, made extremely insulting personal remarks about Robert Hardy's personality, which he had never liked. The management took fright, Robert understandably took grave offence, and all plans to take the show into London were abandoned.

It was another severe blow to my ambitions. Many people have since asked when the show might be revived. The science is still highly relevant, since no one has yet discovered the Theory of Everything, so I have hopes that one day it may be.

CHAPTER NINETEEN

France

I have always had a soft spot for France, nurtured by a couple of childhood camping holidays in Brittany, and even more by a week-long summer vac course in the glamorous town of Cannes on the Cote d'Azur, to which my parents had sent me when I was sixteen.

The Mediterranean coast, with its stunning summer climate, its situation between sea and mountains, and its long history of association with painters, writers, aristocrats, and celebrities of all kinds, famous and infamous, seemed to me the ultimate in sophisticated living.

Once freed from our ties to Tenerife, I suggested to Sheila that we explore this part of the world. We went on a prolonged car tour of Provence and the Riviera.

We soon realised that the Eastern end of the coastline, where stood the well-known cities – Monte Carlo, Nice, Cannes, Villefranche etc – was not for us. The world's accumulated late twentieth century wealth seemed to have gravitated there, and the coastline was a seething mass of cliffside mansions, crammed yacht marinas, crowded beaches, and traffic jams. The further West one went, the more natural and rural became the setting, and – although still busy at the height of the season – the more unspoilt the historic

French villages. Also, the cheaper became the property prices – until that is, one reached the billionaire's refuge of St Tropez.

We meandered along the southern end of Provence, past vineyards and pine forests buzzing with cicadas, inspecting the various hilltop villages where time seemed to have halted. Reminders of Peter Mayle's delightful book, *A Year In Provence,* were everywhere. But the really picturesque places were all either too far from the coast, or too dependent on tourists and holiday homes to provide what we sought. We wanted a real French working village, where one could join a more permanent community than just the fleeting summertime population.

We eventually came across a small place called Roquebrune-sur-Argens, not far from the sea, not too self-conscious, and boasting a golf course. The village centre was a classic collection of steep cobbled streets, old houses, and restaurants clustered round a shady square. The golf course was just outside, and had a housing development under construction beside it.

We went for a bite of lunch at the clubhouse, and asked about the development. The barman pointed across the terrace and said, "That's one of the sales agents there, talking to those people. Ask him."

We waited until his customers had left, and approached him. My French is acceptable, if not fluent, and I asked about the complex, which we could see was comprised of attractive flower-fringed lanes and small villas. The man said in French, "Oh, I'm afraid they're all sold."

"But they're not all built yet," I said.

"Well, no, but there are only six left to build and we have buyers for all of them."

"Can we have a look anyway?"

He gave a Gallic shrug, and took us through the paths to the far edge, where the six unbuilt plots were marked out on a knoll overlooking a vineyard, with wooded hills beyond.

"But this is the best position on the whole site," I said.

He grinned and shrugged again.

I asked, "Are you sure they are all sold?"

"Well, we have people who want them, but they don't all have deposits on them yet."

"If I gave you a deposit now, would you accept it?"

It was almost a repeat of our first Tenerife purchase. The price for a small three-bedroomed house and garden was a mere one hundred thousand euros. I gave him a cheque for ten thousand, and the place was ours.

We had to wait until the following summer to take possession. There followed five years of happy family summers there, highlighted by the typical French pastimes of lunches on the terrace, dinners in the village restaurants under the plane trees, trips to the sea, and of course golf. I wrote various plays and another novel whilst there.

But then, having decided that this region and this lifestyle was for us, we began to consider a more serious commitment to it. The girls had by now left school, were married and producing grand children (more later), and we felt we needed a more substantial property, where the growing family and our various friends and relatives could congregate. We had downsized in Bath, and had a bit more money in the bank. We also knew that area of Provence better.

We had discovered another classic, but little known village some twenty kilometres west of Roquebrune, surrounded by vineyards and pine-covered hills, and only ten minutes drive from the attractive old seaside resort of Ste Maxime on the Bay of St Tropez. Its name was Plan de la Tour (*Plain of the Tower* – although the tower, presumably an old Knight's Templar fortification or some such, was long vanished). Film star Johnny Depp and his partner Vanessa Paradis lived in splendour just outside the village, and George Clooney owned a vineyard not far away.

So began another marathon property search – on a rather humbler scale than theirs. Over the course of two years we investigated dozens of houses, all either too far out of the village, too cramped, or too expensive. Then one day, back in Bath, I received a phone call from one of the French agents, who after several abortive viewings knew what we were looking for.

"I have your house, Robin," she said.

"What do you mean?"

"Zis is ze one. Exactly what you want, and it's on ze edge of ze village. You must come see it."

"We're just about to fly to Australia," I said (a later story).

"Well, it will sell quickly."

That's what all agents say. I took a plane the next day. She was right. It was a typical Provencal villa in a private cul-de-sac, with potential for five spacious bedrooms, three bathrooms, a large garden with lovely swimming pool, and remarkably was only five minutes walk from the village centre.

I called Sheila. She too flew out, and approved. Fortunately the owners didn't want completion for another six months whilst they arranged their move to Marseilles. So we signed the contract and flew to Australia, knowing we had our French home to come back to.

Les Collines, as we called it, became our summer home up until the present day. We converted the garage to a guest suite, put in a second kitchen for guests, added a 'boules' court (obligatory in France), and extended the garden with oleander hedges and lawns all around the pool area, much to the amusement of the French – "You English love your grass!".

The country *route touristique* to the village from the A8 motorway is a dazzling snake of a road along the hillsides, with stunning views and steep drops through the mountain pines. It scares the pants of many visitors, but the tradesman's vans and myself charge around it with the ease of familiarity. The hills are inhabited by lizards, wild boar, and tortoises, and smell of pines and sunshine.

The family join us out there regularly, and friends and relatives from everywhere (even Australia) have found their way there at one time or another. We made friends with French neighbours and villagers, and with many British ex-pats who lived around the area, including several like us coming from Bath. Old acting friends Ken Farrington and James Faulkner had places nearby. And I joined a group of British, American and other nationalities playing weekly golf at the most glorious golf course I know, deep in the local mountains, named *St Endréol.*

Over the years we have found our favourite places to visit across the region – the famous town of Aix-en-Provence, the gorgeous villages of Grimaud, Gassin, and Garde-Freinet, the beaches and sea-front restaurants of Ste Maxime, and of course the ferry rides across the bay to gawp at the tycoons' yachts and wander the enchanting backstreets of St Tropez – once a mere fishing village haunted by all the Impressionist painters, but then made famous when Brigitte Bardot and her husband Roger Vadim moved there in the 50s. (She still lives there on her estate, a wizened old lady devoted to looking after abandoned animals, having given up on men.)

I should deviate here to mention our association with a billionaire – the only really wealthy person we have ever known intimately, and one with connections to the Cote d'Azur.

Frederick Koch was the oldest of four siblings, heirs to the gigantic American Koch fortune, based mostly on oil (what else?), but including railways, pharmaceuticals, mining, property, etc, etc. Koch Industries is reputed to be the second largest privately owned company in America. Fred was the black sheep of the family, being gay and artistically inclined, and leaving the running of the business largely to his two younger brothers (who are to this day the main financial backers of the right-wing Tea Party movement in the US).

We met Fred back in the eighties, through our old friend Derek Fowlds, whom Fred had befriended whilst Derek was playing on Broadway. He took to us as part of his widespread circle of friends in the show business fraternity on both sides of the Atlantic.

Fred was an extraordinary character. Perhaps the most polymathic authority on all the arts I have ever known. He was in his time patron of the Lincoln Arts Centre in New York, the Spoleto and Salzburg Festivals, and the Royal Shakespeare Company –

for which he funded the building of the Swan Theatre. Also of innumerable libraries, arts foundations, and cultural institutions across America. He would come to London every month of June, staying at The Ritz, and going to see practically every play, opera, and ballet production running there – sometimes three events in a day. His collections of rare manuscripts and art works were among the finest in the world.

But his main enterprise was the buying and restoring of fine historic houses.

Over the years, he spent tens of millions renovating in meticulous detail various grand estates around America, and such palaces as Sutton Place (England's second largest Tudor mansion after Hampton Court), Bluhnbach Castle – a vast Hapsburg hunting lodge near Salzburg, and Torre Clementina – an extraordinary Romanesque mansion at Cap St Martin, overlooking the Bay of Monte Carlo.

Over a period of thirty years we met up with Fred at least once a year, when he invited us to lunch at The Ritz, or to stay at Salzburg or Cap St Martin. We even had him to stay at Bath, although the accommodation was never up to his meticulous standards.

He lived alone, having abandoned partnerships as being too problematic, and compensating by socialising with people he found amusing. His routines were lavish and precise. He would always have three full meals a day, cooked by a top chef, hired from wherever he was at the time – and guests were expected to partake equally. He would then conduct a tour round his huge properties (Bluhnbach Castle had forty bedrooms, Torre Clementina had only four, but incredibly lavish – the house was valued at a quarter of a billion dollars!), pointing out various notable items in his art and book collections. He owned many old masters and Impressionist paintings, and original manuscripts such as ancient Bibles, and Shakespeare and Mozart folios. One article at Bluhnbach which I particularly remember was Queen Victoria's Windsor Castle visitors book, which contained the names and signatures of numerous Kings, Queens, Dukes, Prime Ministers, and others. When I asked Fred how he came by it, he just waved a casual hand, and murmured in his camp drawling voice, "Oh, I don't know. My spies found it at some auction or other." Why the Queen let it go, I can't imagine. Perhaps she was hard up. Or just had too many such, and didn't want to be further reminded of all her disreputable relatives.

At the Salzburg Festival – where all those years ago I had attended the production of *The Secret* and missed my chance to seduce Romy Schneider – we were driven by his chauffeur to watch wonderful concerts from front row seats. At Cap Martin we drank champagne beside the most exotic swimming pool I have ever seen. At the Castle of Montegufoni in Tuscany, which Fred was renting from the Sitwell family for the summer, I mixed with a coterie of gay New York intellectuals, whose camp Wildean talk kept me entertained during lavish dinners and drunken wine tasting in the vineyards of the estate.

These were rare samplings of the mega-rich lifestyle. However, although Fred loved to laugh, he never seemed to us a happy man. He rarely stayed for more than a week in any of his European havens, although they were maintained all the year round by large household and gardening staffs. He was always seeking after perfection, and could never relax and enjoy the ordinary, the mundane, the simple pleasures of life. We have not seen him for a while, and he died early this year, 2020, I think in his Fifth Avenue penthouse. Where all his millions have gone I do not know, since he had no immediate family of his own.

I'm glad I'm not a billionaire.

Sheila and I began the custom of driving from Bath to *Les Collines* at the start of each summer, always taking a different route, and over three or four days exploring the superbly preserved towns and villages of inland France, staying in its idyllic converted chateau hotels, tasting the wines, and sampling French cuisine, still at its best the finest in the world (although in many ordinary locations rapidly becoming the poorest. We were surprised to learn that, after America, France is one of the world's largest fast-food locations. The tradition of delicious country bistro-style cooking seems to be disappearing).

Dining out has always been one of our greatest pleasures, and perhaps our only real indulgence. We regularly eat out three or four times a week. I never cease to wonder, when eating at a good restaurant, how the chef manages to turn out such a wealth of delicately flavoured dishes, at precisely the right time, to arrive in front of precisely the right people. It is an art as great as any other. Although, knowing a number of restaurant owners as we do, it is not a job I would envy. The hours are worse than an actor's, and the stresses of keeping good chefs, procuring fresh supplies, training expert waiters, and maintaining elegant tables, is enormous. I once, out of curiosity, added up the number of items necessary to set a table and serve a nice three course dinner for four. The total came to almost a hundred. Miss one and you have a disgruntled customer.

Which reminds me of my own experience as a waiter. I was sixteen, and found a holiday job at a popular roadside restaurant near home in Oxted. I was given the task of serving drinks to a large table, during a Saturday night dinner dance. My first attempt resulted in a collection of full glasses sliding down the tray and onto the bare back of a lady diner. Her scream brought the entire restaurant to a standstill and ended my waiting career abruptly.

I have great admiration for good waiters as well as chefs.

CHAPTER TWENTY

Australia

France has been a joy to us. The dry, sparkling summers of the Riviera are probably the best in the world. However the winters are not so good. The days can be fine and sunny – which is what attracted Queen Victoria and the masses of English and Russian aristocracy who flooded there during the nineteenth and early twentieth century winters – but the nights can be distinctly chilly. Frost and occasional snow are not unknown on the beaches of the Cote d'Azur. When the darkness draws in early in the evening, the tourists retreat, and many of the restaurants and cafes close – and then the villages take on a forlorn air. Ours remains active, being a working village based on its wineries, and some of the restaurants struggle manfully to remain open, but still it can be dismal at night.

We were too conditioned by life in the sun, and wondered what the winter solution might be for our old age.

As it happened, Gemma, our younger daughter solved it for us.

Both she and Lindsay had done a lot of travelling after they left school. They had each taken the traditional time off to go round Europe by hitch-hike, camper van, and whatever other means available. Lindsay in particular had expanded her initial six months to a year, and then two, eventually ending up travelling the African continent (how did we let her do that??). The wandering spirit entered her blood, and led to her voyaging with her future sons at an early age to wild places on every continent. This produced the basis for a long-running travel column in the Sunday Telegraph, and eventually for a career as a remarkable novelist.

But it was Gemma who introduced us to Australia.

About the time that we were first investigating Provence, Gemma was investigating Corfu on one of her own backpacking travels. There she met a young Australian who was also doing a European trip, and they embarked on one of those wild romances without which no summer holiday is complete. She told us a little about it, but we didn't think there was much in it, Australia being a tad too far for continued passion.

However the following year she announced that she was off again, and this time further afield. A round the world trip no less, with Australia as one of the stopping places.

It appeared that he was there to meet her off the plane, and the next thing we knew was that she was engaged to be married, and was going to live in Melbourne.

She was only twenty two, and being extremely attractive, could be selective in her choice of partners. When we suggested that she was still a bit young to get hitched, she pointed out that Sheila had been a year younger then that when I married her, and she was being selective! We had no argument.

We had mixed feelings. On the one hand we would be losing a much loved daughter to the other side of the world. On the other, we had the perfect excuse to go there ourselves and see the Southern hemisphere.

I had always wanted to visit Australia, drawn by the image of bronzed Aussies, foaming surf beaches, vast desert spaces. I had had play productions on there, but had never managed to attend one. We flew out for a long Christmas visit, to investigate both Australia, and her fiancé Paul.

Gemma had suggested that, before going down to Melbourne in the far south where Paul and his family lived, we should first meet up for a seaside holiday in Queensland, twelve hundred miles north. We were to fly to Brisbane and thence drive seventy miles up the coast to a place with the strange Aborigine name of Noosa (meaning shaded).

How could we know that this would become our favourite place on the planet, eclipsing Bath, and Provence, and everywhere else that we had ever visited?

Noosa is the St Tropez of Australia, but with a year round sub-tropical climate. Daytime temperatures range from above 20C in the winter to over 30C in the summer. Sometimes humid in that season, but at least that's kind to the skin. The vegetation is prolific, with a myriad flowering bushes and palms, and majestic tree species, around which fly an exotic and musical population of birdlife.

The area is an astonishing conglomeration of golden beaches, wide river, winding waterways, and large nature parks. Around and amongst all this, are half-hidden millionaires homes, sophisticated shops, superb restaurants, and, as everywhere in Australia, great golf courses. Gemma had put us up in a holiday apartment looking down to a seven mile-long surf beach, in a dune-top village area of Noosa named Sunshine Beach(!)

Twenty years later, I am writing this a mere fifty metres from that same apartment block.

After a sublime couple of weeks in Noosa, by which time we were completely seduced by the place, we flew down to Melbourne to meet Paul and his family.

Melbourne in Victoria is Australia's second city – fiercely rivalrous with Sydney – with over four million inhabitants, and frequently quoted as the world's most liveable town (although this doesn't take into account its very changeable climate). It is situated on the Yarra River and the wide Port Phillip Bay, and its wealth originated in the gold rush of the late nineteenth century. It is an urbane conglomeration of skyscrapers, old Victorian buildings, gastronomic restaurants, and Australia's finest collection of sports facilities – playing host to their tennis open, golf open, grand prix, and top events in horse-racing, cricket, rugby, etc.

Paul lived South of the city, where a number of pleasant suburbs spread down the eastern shores of the bay towards the vineyards, forests, and golf courses of the Mornington Peninsular. We were to get to know the area well over the coming years, it becoming almost a second Australian home for us.

Paul's family turned out to be Dutch émigrés who welcomed us into their circle of friends with enthusiasm. Paul's father, Roel, ran a thriving tiling and tile shops business, and was a leading light amongst the thirty thousand strong Melbourne Dutch community. Paul himself had all his parents' warmth and charm (though not their Dutch accents), and we took to him happily as a future member of our own family.

Through regular visits to Victoria over the years, during which we rented or house-swapped in various locations around the sea and countryside, we accumulated long-standing friendships with a number of Australians and British ex-pats, as well as getting to know Gemma and Paul's wide social circle.

We also got to know much about the Australian character.

Broadly speaking, the French are quiet, amicable, insular, defensive, and resistant to change. They make good friends, but resentful enemies. NEVER get into legal proceedings in France if you can help it. Their laws are antiquated and indecipherable, and everyone comes out damaged, poorer, and a good deal older.

Australians on the other hand are noisy, outgoing, entrepreneurial, sports mad, and widely travelled. They are extremely sociable, and on the whole very efficient business-wise. Also law-abiding, despite their criminal 'Botany Bay' origins. They always stop at a pedestrian crossing, even when you are ten yards from it. The French won't stop unless they are about to run you down. The Spanish won't stop anyway.

Australians are an odd mixture of boldness and prudery. Australian girls will happily walk down famous Hastings Street in Noosa, in the tiniest bikinis you've ever seen, but they won't go topless on the beach like French girls.

Most white Australians, whilst highly chauvinistic, will trace their ancestry back to the UK, and still show great interest in British political and social events. They were deeply hurt when Britain abandoned Australasia's trade for Europe's in the 1970s, and are eager to re-establish the ties, post Brexit. Many older residents are actually British in origin, but have settled in Australia after careers around the Commonwealth, in South Africa, Honk Kong, Singapore, etc.

The country is heavily influenced by America, but I am always surprised by how much it exhibits its ties to 'the old country', still utilising the British systems of governance, broadcasting BBC programmes over its radio and TV stations, and involving itself with widespread British cultural, business and scientific affairs.

This attachment shows itself through the fascination Australians have with the Royal Family, and the rejection of proposed republican reform whenever referendums are held – although this may eventually change.

Many of their towns and place names are echoes of British ones. However I do love their Aborigine names – Mooloolaba, Woolloongabba, Bong Bong, Woolloomooloo. They all mean something, but don't ask me what.

Australia seems to have got things as near right as possible in this imperfect world. It is indeed 'the lucky country'. My main criticism is that it is rather prone to the nanny state mentality. This was demonstrated during the Corona pandemic, when all the state premieres rushed to close their borders as if they were European countries about to be invaded by Hitler. This didn't prevent any extra infections nationwide, but it almost caused inter-state warfare. As I write, there have been only a few hundred deaths over the entire sub-continent, a fraction of those elsewhere, or caused by flu and road accidents. Meanwhile many Australian businesses and the economy are hitting a brick wall, along with the rest of the world.

We began the annual practice of travelling down-under as soon as the European winter approached, basing ourselves in Noosa, but flying regularly to Melbourne, curtesy of Australia's cheap inland airways. We sometimes did the journey by road down the eastern seaboard, stopping off at small surfside towns, often built around the frequent river estuaries.

Lindsay and her boys have managed to join us from England every couple of years, and they and their Australian cousins love the Noosa environment as much as we do – especially for the swimming and surfing.

Ah, surfing.

I envy the childhood experience here. Sunshine Beach boasts one of the country's finest surf-clubs – another unique Australian institution, developed from the original basic shacks for the life guards that patrol every major beach, to large bar/restaurant complexes with the best positions on the coastline. They also house the collections of speed-boats, jet skis, and other sophisticated equipment that is used nowadays for life saving. With so much leisure time spent amongst the continent's waves, the annual death toll is considerable.

But it is all part of the youth culture from a very early age. Droves of young kids can be seen after conventional lessons, down on the sand in their bright surf-club colours, learning to swim, sail, surf and life-save. They don't know how lucky they are.

And it seems a lifetime passion. It is not unusual to see grizzled seventy, and even eighty year-old men, trotting barefoot down to the beach with their surf-boards under their arms, when the waves are up.

I have always had a fascination for the surfing culture, ever since my elementary teenage attempts during Cornish holidays. Even in my forties I subscribed to a surfing magazine, hypnotised by the photos of surfers 'tubing' the amazing waves in Hawaii and Indonesia. One of our local restauranteurs was an ex-champion surfer, and he showed me photos of surf riders as tiny dots riding one hundred foot-high waves off the coast of Portugal!

Either incredibly brave or incredibly foolish.

After renting apartments in Sunshine Beach for the first two or three years, we decided that we wanted to make our association with the country permanent, so we started looking for a property to buy. We also commenced the long, complex business of obtaining permanent residents visas. The days of the 'Ten pound Pom' were long gone. Australia is now very protective of its immigration rules, since refugees and expats from many nations seek to settle there. We initially had to obtain limited holiday visas each year, but eventually, after much bureaucracy and a considerable outlay in cash, we procured our residencies, which allowed us to stay as long as we wished, and also to take advantage of the superb Australian health system (which Britain would do well to emulate).

We began our regular house-hunting procedure – or in this case flat hunting. We had experienced enough of maintaining large properties, and in any case still had the French house to look after.

The Australian property scene is intriguing. Just as prone to price fluctuations as everywhere else, but very dependent on situation. Everyone wants to live on or close to the sea, unless they are wedded to the land and to rural pursuits, in which case they want large acreage with access to water. Places overlooking the sea, or on the wide rivers, as many are in Sydney and Brisbane, can fetch double those elsewhere.

And this is the same in Noosa as everywhere else. There are a plethora of magnificent houses ranged across the top of the high dunes, or lining the inland waterways, with their private boat jetties at the end of the garden. And around Sunshine Beach, our own favoured area, these mingle with small apartment blocks, never more than three stories high, but all boasting spacious units, sun terraces, and communal swimming pools.

The architecture can be exotic, ranging from pseudo-Victorian mansions to space-age edifices from a Star Wars set. Because there is so much space and little planning constriction, architects are free to use their wildest imaginations.

European homes are designed mostly from the outside in, being confined within traditional period terraces and houses. The rooms have to conform to the outer facades and window arrangements. In Australia however one can build from scratch, from the inside out. Therefore designs start with the owner's preferences – for an open plan lounge area here, a bedroom suite there, a recreation area somewhere else. Garages go underneath, vast windows take in the views in whichever direction desired, balconies and terraces sprout on all sides, gardens and pools wind around, under, and between the various wings of the place. Foreigners often stare in bewilderment at the fantastic glass, steel, and stone sculpted creations. But once inside one realises the ingenuity behind it all – every room making the most of light, views, and space.

We were determined to get at least a three-bedroomed apartment at Sunshine Beach, with enough accommodation for families and friends. The palatial penthouse creations with sea views were out of our reach. However, after viewing a mind-numbing selection of properties, and just before flying back to the UK (in our usual last minute fashion), we discovered a ground floor apartment in a residential block only half a stone's throw from the small parade of shops and restaurants which led down to the beach.

The flat was slightly worn, and had just the smallest of sea glimpses through a copse of trees, so it was reasonably priced. But it had more space even than usual, and access to a superb communal pool – essential for our daily swim, always part of our keep fit regime. It also had that rarest of features, a garden patch in front.

We were fortunate in that the pound was strong against the dollar at that time, and we bought it for the equivalent of £200,000. We have spent the Australian summers there ever since.

We may even die there.

CHAPTER TWENTY ONE

More Writing and More Heartaches

In recent years, with a backlog of comedies behind me, I have tended to write more serious stuff.

Before the Corona pandemic struck, I had high hopes for a play about Winston Churchill and the Second World War. I had come across an extraordinary incident that happened during the first few weeks of the war, when Churchill and his wife, Clementine, invited the Prime Minister, Neville Chamberlain and his wife, Anne, to dinner at Admiralty House. The two men had been at daggers drawn for years over the appeasement issue, which had kept Churchill out of the government for a decade, and this was the first and only time the four had met socially. There is no record as to what happened during that unique evening. So I decided to write a play about it.

It is titled *The Lion & The Unicorn.* After some time trying to attract the right star to play Churchill, and being turned down by all the obvious people who had already done him, I and the producers staged a rehearsed reading at the Prince of Wales Theatre in London, to which we invited various interested parties. This is always a gamble, as one never knows quite how the reading will go. However, we had a great cast, including Michael Maloney as

Churchill, Jane Asher as his wife, friends Simon Williams and his wife Lucy Fleming as the Chamberlains, and my old colleague from RADA, Donald Douglas, as the Churchill's butler, playing chorus to the piece. They were all splendid, considering that they had only been through the play a couple of times, and Michael especially gave a marvellous Churchill impression. The small audience of producers and friends was immensely complimentary, and once again I had hopes of future development.

Then Covid struck, and theatres all over the world closed their doors.

I decided to stick to writing novels for the time being. I had already followed *A Rustle In The* Grass with an ambitious novel inspired by a wonderful biography of Charles Darwin's wife, Emma, written by Edna Healey (wife of the Labour Chancellor, Dennis Healey). It described in fascinating detail the loving Darwin household during Charles's productive years, during which Emma played a vital role.

It has always been my belief that Darwin's theory of evolution was the most crucial scientific discovery ever made, explaining as it does how the world and all its species – and indeed the universe itself – evolved. My book, *Survival Of The Fittest*, is a modern day detective story, in which an eccentric London antiquarian book seller is hired by an equally eccentric American billionaire to hunt down, both Emma Darwin's fictitious private diary, and a hitherto unpublished postscript to her husband's vast body of work, in which he explains his views about religion.

I have always puzzled over the way the religious instinct still endures amongst the most developed and educated populations on the planet (and more so amongst the undeveloped ones). As Darwin himself explains, the belief seems to be hard-wired into man's psyche, a legacy from his primitive origins when he needed to trust in an all-powerful paternal authority – God the 'Father' – to make sense of an anarchic world.

However, surely now there is enough evidence to show that no such guiding light exists. If it did, why is there still such a profusion of differing beliefs in its form, such a dearth of progress in halting the litany of cruelty and corruption throughout history, and such widespread evidence of injustice in people's lives, where the good suffer terrible tragedy, and the bad go unpunished? Why is it that so many vicious conflicts rely on a plethora of deities to justify each side's cause – Protestant v Catholic, Christian v Muslim, Muslim v Hindu, Shia v Sunni? Wouldn't a real God have sorted this out by now? Or is it that there are a whole gang of gods fighting amongst themselves?

And before anyone says, well it's all down to man's own freedom of choice, then the answer has to be, then why pray to a God at all?

The Greek philosopher Epicurus put it in a nutshell over two thousand years ago:-

'If God is willing, but not able, then he is not omnipotent.
If he is able, but not willing, then he is not benevolent.
If he is both able and willing, then whence cometh evil?
If he is neither able nor willing, then why call him God?'

Even more naïve, it seems to me, is the Christian belief in Jesus as the 'son' of God. One only has to ask three questions:

1. If God did send him down to earth to put things right for

homo sapiens, why did he wait over two hundred thousand years of man's existence to do so?

2. Why did he send the 'Messiah' to an obscure desert tribe, where he would have little global impact, rather than to a major political centre such as Rome, Athens, or Alexandria, where his message might truly resound (no, Jerusalem was not such)?

3. And again, why has Christ, for all his admirable moral orations, had so little effect in driving them home where they are most needed? How is his hideous death supposed to 'atone' for everyone else's sins? Seriously?

Man is still at heart a primitive being, for all his technical skills. He still hankers for someone or something to take control of a chaotic existence. But that, it seems to me, is to evade responsibility. It is putting the onus on God's shoulders, not his own.

Survival Of The Fittest is published on Amazon, and has received a number of gratifying five star reviews, but has never made it to the best seller lists.

More recently I decided to write something aimed directly at the mass market. A political thriller titled *Number Ten,* in the full-blown style of John Grisham, Jeffrey Archer, et al, with all the political intrigue, gangster conflict, and romantic crisis I could devise. By now I seriously needed a literary agent to promote it since my theatre agent, Brendan Davis, does not deal with books.

I received regretful rejections from various London agents. Then one wrote back, saying she thought it was a terrific thriller, and she couldn't put it down. However she wouldn't take it on, as she didn't know how to find a publisher for it!

I was up against the modern obstacle of far too many titles out there, few of them having any hope of selling unless they are by prize-winning writers or already established best-sellers. This has been caused largely by the abolition of price control on literature, and by the e-book revolution, whereby anyone can now self-publish through Amazon, offering their books for 99p or less. Discovering the good stuff amongst the vast mass of rubbish is very difficult.

However, having self-published *Number Ten* myself, it has now gone on to gather another list of glowing reviews, and to be short-listed for a minor thriller prize. My screenplay based on it is perfect for a Netflix film or series, so one never knows.

I have also written a novel based on the Churchill play, but with a much-expanded scenario. And an ambitious literary story spanning the last half century, titled *A Perfect Being*.

Well, it keeps the grey cells going, and me out of mischief.

Back in Bath, we had over the years gradually downsized as we spent less and less time there. We had moved to Ashlands, a lovely Italianate villa with far-reaching views to the Westbury White Horse, which was Sheila's favourite of all our houses. Thence, after our customary seven years, to a penthouse apartment in Warleigh Manor, a converted mansion in the countryside outside the city. And finally we ended up right in the centre of Bath, to a smallish two bed flat in an extraordinary building called The Empire.

This great block, standing with the River Avon on one side, and Bath Abbey on the other, was built in 1899 as Bath's first luxury hotel. Over the next hundred years it served variously as an exotic watering hole for wealthy Edwardians, then during World War II and beyond, as the main administrative offices for the Ministry of Defence, and finally as a block of elegant apartments for the elderly (well, over 55s, which surely isn't elderly these days).

Astonishingly, through all those transitions, it has managed to preserve its original period opulence, with plush red carpets, vast mahogany staircases, cornices, chandeliers, and classical paintings on the walls. It still retains its main lounge and dining room for the use of residents, and the basement boasts guest suites, cinema, gymnasium, sauna, and full-sized billiards room. As our UK pied-a-terre, where we only reside now for three months in the year, it is ideal – like the luxury hotel that we can't afford. It's a stone's throw from all the city's amenities, and perfectly situated for friends to drop by, and for Lindsay and the boys to use as their city centre rendezvous whenever we are home.

Lindsay, our eldest daughter, had by now finally landed, after a much-travelled life, in a lovely apartment overlooking country views on the southern outskirts of the city. It is in a large converted paper mill that was reputed to have once been used to print the country's bank notes, and the refined artist's paper used by Gainsborough, Constable, Turner and their like.

Lindsay, before her major travels, had been a student at the Stratford-on-Avon drama college, but had soon realised that following in her parents' theatrical footsteps was not for her. However, whilst there she had met a handsome fellow student, Vaughan, with whom she fell in love. They eventually set up home together on Wimbledon Common, close to her babyhood home at The Keir.

Vaughan was a charming and talented young man, with ambitions as both an actor and a writer. We were very fond of him, and I hope he of us. However, as so often happens in the business, he had extremely bad luck in those early years. He came close to success on several occasions – flying out to Hollywood to film test for George Lucas for the lead in the later Star Wars films, and for Tom Hanks in another movie – and also with various TV and film-script ideas. In the end none of it quite worked, and I know the immense frustration he must have felt during that time. He and Lindsay had to survive mostly on her earnings as a travel writer, and with a little help from us. They eventually got married (at an idyllic summer wedding and reception held in our Bath garden), and had two children, Dow and Orly, separated by almost three years.

However fate intruded again, and the marriage sadly ended while the children were still young. Lindsay was devastated, but eventually came through it all. We helped by flying them all out to Australia, and giving them regular long holidays over the years at the French house, but in the end the burden of raising the boys rested on her shoulders.

Over the following decade, she and her sons lived in various rural corners of England, and travelled to all corners of the earth in the course of her travel writing, during which she home-schooled the boys. They may have missed out on a bit of orthodox education, but they must be the most worldly children on the planet, and they are both growing up to be extraordinary people.

A supplement to Lindsay's story is that she has progressed

from journalism to being a serious novelist in her own right. She has a vivid imagination and a unique poetic style. Her first novel, *Jacob's Colours*, so excited agents and publishers that she was paid an extraordinary one hundred thousand pounds advance for it, certainly more than I ever achieved. We are waiting for her to win her first major prize.

As a father I find it hard to be objective, but both Lindsay and Gemma are strikingly beautiful, warm and charismatic people, with legions of friends in all corners of the planet. Gemma meanwhile has also become a writer, but in this case a copy writer. She has built up a solo business working mostly from home, and designs websites and copy for a number of businesses large and small. She and Paul and their two dazzling children have a nice house south of Melbourne centre, just a few hundred metres from the village of Black Rock and the beaches of Port Phillip Bay. All four grand children are exceedingly clever and sporty.

Where they all get it from I'm not sure. Must be Sheila.

CHAPTER TWENTY TWO

Dark and Light

As I have said, luck, chance, fate, play an immense part in most people's lives. There is no doubt that, despite the disappointments, I have been remarkably lucky.

I was part of a generation that has on the whole been prosperous, and has never had to experience global war – despite my own early fatherless years during World War II, which I suspect had quite a profound subconscious impact.

I was born into the most civilised nation on earth – and when you have experienced many others, you come to realise that. Britain has paved the way for most of the successful countries of the Western world – with its democratic values, its parliamentary procedures, its respect for law and order, and its pride in itself (until recently). I am always surprised when abroad to discover how much foreigners still admire Britain for its examples, its history, its capabilities, and its culture (and of course its Royal Family). It's a shame the British themselves don't do the same.

I was given from birth a constitution and healthy metabolism that has served me well for a lifetime – supported by a daily exercise regime. I am the same weight at eighty as I was at eighteen, and I can still run a hundred yards in around sixteen seconds. (Mind you, doing a parachute jump from 15000 feet to celebrate my eightieth birthday was overdoing it a bit. The scariest thing I've ever done!)

I have, in spite of the disappointments and my own inadequacies, discovered a career that has given me huge satisfaction until this day, and also as pleasant a lifestyle as I could wish for – although, as I write, the covid pandemic is closing theatres around the world, which is causing something of a hiccup.

I found a wife, who, despite all the strains and stresses imposed on her, has kept the family together, and our love alive for over fifty years. We still like each other's company best. She too is busy writing, and is wonderful at keeping up with all the family, and at fostering social circles in our various places. Most of our friends are now from worlds far removed from show business – worlds ostensibly more sane and stable.

And above all, I was born innately happy. As I said at the beginning of this book, one of the factors that makes for happiness is one's primary biological makeup. My younger brother, Christopher, was not so lucky. Despite being intelligent, likeable and good-looking, he was prone to black periods of despair, and his life ended tragically in his early thirties. However, he left behind two immensely talented and successful children, Amanda and Adam, so his legacy endures.

Yes, a lot of it is the luck of the draw.

And certainly, not all is music and sunshine. There are many things that make me angry or disappointed with the world.

Primary amongst them being mankind's stupidity. I am no genius, but the scale of human folly across the planet continues to astound me. It displays itself through every new headline, and every new atrocity. From political despotism, to religious fanaticism, to criminal obsession, the evidence of man's bestial instincts still persists everywhere – even as he simultaneously creates the most inspiring works of art and the most ingenious scientific inventions.

As Einstein said – "Only two things are infinite. The universe and man's stupidity. And I'm not sure about the former."

And Voltaire – "The number of those who think is exceedingly small, and they are not interested in upsetting the world."

And Churchill – "The best argument against democracy is five minutes conversation with the average voter."

If one ever needed proof, just look at the vote of Americans – supposedly the most affluent and sophisticated people on the planet – for the most boorish and disreputable president they've ever had (although, as I write, he seems to be on the way out).

And at a humbler domestic level, there are things which make me angry. I will list some of them.

POLITICS AND THE MEDIA

Most politicians are actually intelligent and hard-working people (despite what Chris Patten says). They wouldn't get past the selection process if they weren't – at least in the UK, where it's pretty reliable. They could all be earning several times an MP's salary out in civvy street. Yes, the power imperative exists, but it's rarely excessive in a democratic system. Most politicians are just there to try and make a difference, even if they often seem to lack vision.

Once upon a time the approach of media interviewers and commentators was to show respect for a politician's status, and interrogate them with a view to discovering what they actually thought about an issue. In recent decades however, especially with the advent of the celebrity TV interviewer, the aim has become to attack, to embarrass, and to catch out their subject with obscure statistics and quotes from some speech they made five years ago. Presenters have forgotten that they are mere hack journalists whose job is to act as intermediaries between us and the interviewee, and instead act like demagogues, parading their own prejudices, constantly interrupting and accusing, as if they are the real stars and they know better than whoever is in front of them. They are answerable to no one, and nothing except the viewing figures. It is all power and no responsibility.

I think this cynicism is causing insidious damage to the democratic system, and the public's attitude towards their governments.

That said, the politicians own raucous behaviour in Parliament does not help. Why the British Parliament does not enforce the normal rules of debate, whereby everyone keeps quiet until a person has finished speaking, I cannot understand.

DRUGS

The drugs industry is by far the largest criminal activity on the planet, almost rivalling the oil business in turnover. It is responsible for tragedy, poverty, and ruined lives on a gigantic scale. It destroys economies, societies, and entire countries. Yet governments continually mishandle it.

Narcotics in one form or another have been an addiction since the beginning of time, certainly way beyond the ancient Greek and Roman civilisations. It is clear that this is built into the human

DNA (like religion). Man will always find ways to use opiates and other stimulants to relieve his burdens.

Once this is accepted, then the solution is obvious. There is no point in trying to legislate against their use. That simply hands the whole business into the hands of the criminals, as happened in the last century with alcohol. Surely prohibition taught us that.

The answer therefore is for governments to take over and legalise the industry themselves. They can then control sales, maintain quality control (most criminally sold drugs are falsified or impure), limit drug abuse via prescription, institute a system of education as has been done so successfully with tobacco, and finally utilise the profits for the tax-payer, instead of giving them to the gangsters. The income would probably cover the entire National Health budget.

Portugal effectively decriminalised drug possession twenty years ago. Its death rate from them is now one fifth of the European average, and one fiftieth of the US.

However, whenever such a suggestion is made public, the outcry is deafening. The instinct to try and legislate against malign influences, instead of managing them, is as ever dominant.

COMPULSIONS

I am fortunate in not having an addictive temperament. I know that when I eat too much, drink too much, smoke too much, I will pay the price later on. I have never experienced genuine addiction, am unqualified to comment. However, when I see the havoc that the conscious attachment to drink, drugs, smoking, eating, or gambling wreaks on people's lives, I do wonder at the lack of self-control. Is man really such an impotent animal? In Australia, half the population are keep-fit fanatics. The other half are as indulgent as anywhere else, bingeing on beer and huge platefuls of carbohydrates, and parading their obesity for all to see.

It's easy to stay healthy. A banana, a glass of champagne, and fifteen minutes of serious exercise a day, and you'll live for ever!

Again, today's hypnotic fixation on the smart phone and the social media strikes me as one of the most destructive threats to society in the modern era. Young people especially are living vicariously through their obsession with the small screen. They are missing out on what is really going on around them, and the effect on their mental health is now well-documented.

I do have a mobile, but my family always complain because it's never turned on.

NATIONAL HEALTH

The British National Health system, once the envy of the world, is now a disgrace. We have experience of the Spanish, French and the Australian systems, and they are all far superior, whatever the statistics say. The idea of having to wait months for a serious operation would provoke rebellion in most developed countries.

The reason is simple. In most other nations, those who can afford it pay a contribution towards their basic treatment. Usually around 30%, unless unemployed or on benefits. They can take out modest insurance to cover this if they wish. Patients therefore are much more involved with the process. They want value for money, they don't miss appointments (the bane of every British GP surgery), they expect good service, and they get it. It is a partial transaction between patient and provider, and both sides benefit. The friendly, efficient, and happy atmosphere in most surgeries and hospitals abroad, contrasts greatly with the stressed and urgent air at home.

The great British innovation introduced by Nye Bevan back in the forties, stating that 'everything must be free for everyone at point-of-need', was ground-breaking. However it has now become a sacred cow, lifting all responsibility from the patient's shoulders, placing it onto the nanny state, and posing an impossible financial burden on the whole system.

But no politician dares to voice this truth because of the hysterical uproar it would invoke.

EDUCATION

There has been a trend in recent years for left-wing and politically correct prejudices to dominate amongst teachers in the classroom (and often in the universities). This is worrying. The education of the next generation needs to be wise, informed, and impartial. This is our future. Young people should be taught all sides of every issue, and allowed to make up their own minds on philosophies, politics, and morality. Instead a biased attitude seems to prevail amongst the teaching fraternity, aimed at conditioning youth to follow particular prejudices. Many educators appear to lack comprehensive learning themselves. Perhaps we don't pay them enough.

This doesn't seem to be so prevalent in the private sector. Maybe that is why people make such sacrifices to send their children there.

SUPERSTITION

I have already stated my thoughts on religion. However man's superstitious beliefs extend to other less fundamental fields. We know perfectly rational people who won't pass someone on the stairs, who believe that a cracked mirror or spilt salt is a harbinger of disaster, who refuse to plan an event for Friday 13th, who seriously fear that whistling in a dressing room or a mention of the word 'Macbeth' is going to herald a catastrophe.

At a deeper level, the superstitious instinct conditions people's behaviour in all sorts of subconscious or coercive ways. The myriad illogical phobias, the belief in conspiracy theories, the followings of David Icke and his ludicrous preachings that alien lizards are running the world, the panic that the Corona pandemic will mean you'll run out of toilet paper (which in many cases ensured that happened!).

Then there are the herd movements which are a form of superstition – the 'woke' extremists, the political correctness ranters, the Extinction Rebellion panickers, the transgender activists, etc, etc.

And of course, the conviction that the words of the Bible or the Koran are inviolable statutes, somehow dictated by an invisible authority – which has led to untold oppressions and violations.

Excuse me while I go and walk under a ladder.

BREXIT

The level of hysteria, panic, aggression, and downright idiocy over the four years and more of the Brexit process was mind-blowing. The entire British nation went into a paroxysm of self-defeating and infantile frenzy such as it had never known before, while the rest of the world watched in wonder. Parliament dissolved into prehistoric warfare, with attempts on all sides to subvert the democratic process. Older statesman, such as past prime ministers, deputy prime ministers, attorney generals, party leaders and others, who all should have known better, went purple-faced onto the TV screens proclaiming the end of the world. News readers and interviewers obsessed over it like drug-addicted zombies. And the more impressionable members of the public lost their reasoning powers altogether (see Superstition above). As I write, the process is continuing, although partially eclipsed by the Corona crisis, which has produced almost the same amount of hysteria, this time on a global scale.

When will mankind learn that, whatever the predicament, people will eventually deal with it, provided they are shown wise leadership (different from dictatorship), and when their own ingenuity and instinct for self-preservation are given free reign?

DRIVING

I am always irritated by bad driving.

Most people on the roads don't really know how to handle a car. They just use it to get from A to B, and don't much think about it. They brake and accelerate at the wrong times, they enter bends at the wrong angle, they don't read traffic situations. Hence they often make nervous drivers and passengers.

But if you enjoy the challenge of using a modern motor car, then it becomes a matter of learning the skills.

Like Toad of Toad Hall, I have always felt the thrill of the open road. Ever since my old gangster Vauxhall gave up the ghost after being hammered around the highways of provincial Britain, I have owned modestly fast cars of many different marks – always bought second hand. From early MGBs, to Triumph Vitesses, to a monster Toyota Sports that was the first car I had which could comfortably cruise at a hundred on the motorway. Early in my twenties I started taking lessons in rally driving, but I soon realised that I had neither the money nor the time for such a demanding pastime. However it was useful instruction in keeping a car on the road at speed. I did experience the usual skids and bumps during my wilder young days, but I haven't had an accident now for over fifty years, and fingers crossed never will.

We went through the usual array of family cars and station wagons when the children were young, but then we graduated to the BMW scene, and have never left it. In general, BMWs are driver's cars, firm of steering and suspension, clinging to the roads and corners like limpets. Whereas Mercedes and the like are passenger's cars – smooth and quiet and solid. We now possess a ten year-old BMW 3.5 turbo-charged cabriolet, the finest car I've ever driven. We bought it especially for the drives to France, where it eats up the roads with sublime effortlessness, and where the metal roof magically disappears at the press of a button to let the Mediterranean sun pour in. I wish we had one like it here in Australia, but as their restrictive regulations preclude any serious driving, there wouldn't be much point.

And as for the prospect of driverless cars... Is there anything that human beings won't be able to do for themselves in the future? Will we soon have self-operating toilet paper?

MODERN ART

The nonsense that is promoted as 'art' by such as Charles Saatchi and the Tate Modern makes one despair of the human race. Anyone now can splash some daubs on a bit of canvas, pile some bricks into a heap, or dance naked in front of a video camera, and call it art. Anyone can put a meaningless jumble of words together and call it poetry. Anyone can compose a discordant clash of sounds and call it music. The old masters of the arts could dream up any of that stuff in ten minutes. Most modern 'artists' couldn't produce one of their great works in a hundred years. (I exclude David Hockney, who is terrific.)

TELEVISION

I can't stand TV commercials, or 'reality' programmes, or the screaming audiences and judges on the talent shows. Apparently many viewers love them.

Enough of an old man's grousing. I'm off to pour myself that glass of champagne.

Postscript

As I write now, the human race seems to be in its most dismal state for a long time. The Corona pandemic, apart from killing large numbers of people, is causing a global economic disaster that will take decades to recover from.

On top of that, climate change is obsessing the doom-mongers, and the demagogues of the world appear to be on the ascendant – especially in Russia and China.

However, the pendulum always swings. I am a firm believer in ultimate progress. Despite all the incompetence, cruelty, and perversity affecting it, the human species has come a long way since it left the primeval slime, and has achieved stupendous things. Provided it doesn't wipe itself out through misuse of its own technological wizardry, it will continue to advance. The ecological and medical problems will be solved, the money will keep circulating, the despots will fail. We know what happened to communism in the seventies. Even China's seemingly unstoppable progress will expire. No nation that oppresses and restricts its own citizenry to such an extent, whilst simultaneously antagonising the rest of the world, ever lasts for long.

Darwin's revolutionary notion that the fittest ultimately out-survive the unfit is a universal truth that applies everywhere.

Mankind may some day end, as do all species. But the universe will continue.

Acknowledgements

Mostly to my wife, who survived all the trials and challenges I threw at her, and helped me survive them myself.

But also to all the others, too numerous to name, who were instrumental in assisting my successful enterprises, and weathering the unsuccessful ones.

Other Works by Robin Hawdon

A Rustle In The Grass

"It's wonderful – a celebration of hope and courage and dignity in the face of destruction..."

Survival Of The Fittest

"Brilliantly written, extensively researched, it goes deep into the doubts and motivations that eventually lead Charles Darwin to a final decision."

Charlie Poon's Pomes

"A vibrant, hugely entertaining book that adults and children can share and enjoy together."

Number Ten

"A glorious thriller that kept me enthralled throughout."

(Amazon reviews)

Many plays and other works.

Find all on www.robinhawdon.com

Lightning Source UK Ltd.
Milton Keynes UK
UKHW020745250822
407828UK00012B/1653